An opin

LONDON WALKS

Written by
TOM HOWELLS

INFORMATION IS DEAD.
LONG LIVE OPINION.

When we conceived these guidebooks, we feared they would fail. Who needs a guidebook when everything can be googled for free?

But then it occurred to us; that's exactly why you *do* want a guidebook. You want lively, trustworthy opinion combined with great photographs. You don't want endless information from a thousand online bots.

We think you are like us: you care about quality, you care about style, you care about provenance, but you don't have time to waste on long words like 'provenance'. You want to cut to the chase: where's good?

If you were to come and stay on our couch (it's a metaphor btw; we have a guide to hotels), these are the places we'd recommend.

Ann & Martin, co-founders
Hoxton Mini Press

Clerkenwell and Beyond (no.2)
Opposite: South Bank to the City (no.13)

Both images: Hampstead and the Heath (no.19)

BEST FOOT FORWARD

It might not be obvious at first, but London is a walker's city. Sure, the Tube network is a comprehensive web and a wild achievement in engineering – but it's crowded, noisy and grotesquely hot in the summer.

No, this sprawling metropolis was made for *stomping*. I've been a Londoner for two full decades, and the oppressive fug of city living has long been made more enjoyable by simply getting out and exploring the beautiful and bonkers things on offer – things you can't experience while sweltering on the Central line or sitting in traffic on the 176 to Penge. But this breath of fresh air is only the start. Walking is free. It's sustainable. It's healthy. More than anything – hiking in a hailstorm notwithstanding – putting one foot in front of the other and heading out into the world is overwhelmingly fun.

Think of this book as enabling your inner *flâneur*: a wide-eyed observer, idly wandering the city, soaking up its culture and ambience as a means of countering the sometimes apathetic anonymity of the urban environment.

Travelling slowly forces us to engage with our environment in a more profound way than simply whizzing from point to point. Walking encourages wanderlust on a micro scale. By moving at a meditative pace, you notice more of the city's minutiae, whether reading the plentiful blue plaques immortalising its residents, admiring a building's facade or stopping to consider the fecund ecosystems of its many green spaces.

Crucially, pounding the streets also makes London feel *smaller*. We might think of the Tube as a kind of clunky teleportation device: we descend into the urban bedrock, then emerge at our destination with no demonstrable sense of where we are, the route we took to get there or how these places are related. Walking stitches the city together.

Each route in this book comes with carefully compiled directions and a map (to load this on your phone, check the back flap where there is a scannable QR code for each walk). The instructions are intended to be helpful but not restrictive; we'd encourage exploring anything extra that piques your interest along the way. In a cosmopolis like ours, those distractions are pretty much guaranteed.

We might be a culture transfixed by faceless online recommendations and Citymapper, but walking makes a virtue of getting lost. This book isn't gospel; there's nothing like serendipitously stumbling upon something great. We hope you do just that. So lace up, pack a mac if necessary, and hit these terrific trails.

Tom Howells
London, 2025

Tom Howells is a journalist and editor who has written for the *Financial Times*, *Vogue*, *Country Life*, *The Quietus*, *The Fence*, *World of Interiors*, *Wallpaper**, London Design Festival and more. He's an avid walker, both urban and rural, but this book's average of 24,000 steps a day seems quite enough.

BEST FOR...

High summer
Cosmopolitan village vibes, alfresco swimming and a city panorama from Parliament Hill... Hampstead and the Heath (no.19) is a heavenly day out. Meanwhile, A Royal Parks Ramble (no.18) boasts floating pelicans, surprisingly wild tracts of greenery and gleaming palaces.

Winter days
The boozers, gutsy French grub and raunchy neon signage of Soho (no.3) is better enjoyed on chillier, darker days. As is an atmospheric jaunt around the bookish hotspots of Blooms-bury (no.4) – especially those associated with Dickens, a man synonymous with crackling fires and Christmas.

Old-world charm
London's Square Mile (no.1) is brimming with quirky his-toric details: divine churches, storied pubs and even a buried Roman temple. Greenwich may be packed with big hitters like the Cutty Sark and Royal Observatory, but the neighbour-hood is also chock-full of lesser-known historic curios (no.14).

Walking with children
Both the Parkland Walk (no.20) and Little Venice to Camden Lock (no.16) routes are compact enough to be achievable for little legs. The first is replete with dinky wildlife, an eerie

Spriggan and an excellent lunchtime sandwich; the second features colourful houseboats, a floating puppet theatre, monkeys and a killer ice cream to finish.

Fabulous flora

The stretch of the Green Chain from Crystal Palace to Nunhead (no.9) is one of the most bucolic areas of London, while Richmond Park (no.11) offers unkempt wilds and sculpted gardens (the Isabella Plantation is especially irresistible).

Awesome architecture

An amble from South Bank to the City (no.13) takes in geometric post-war concrete and futuristic structures. The Clerkenwell and Beyond route (no.2) includes the grandiose Barbican Centre plus other superlative builds in Sadler's Wells, Spa Green and Smithfields.

Getting your steps in

Wandering the Thames Path from Wandsworth to Kew (no.15) is almost a full day out if you factor a leisurely lunch and Kew Gardens at its culmination. Or you can tackle the Thames in the other direction, slaloming the seven esteemed bridges from Putney to Waterloo (no.17).

Escaping the smog

The pastoral dreamscape of Epping Forest feels a world away from central London – and this circular route (no.8) is a perfect way to experience it. Alternatively, The Lea River (no.7) offers sleepy towpaths and lovely reaches of urban wetland.

1

THE SQUARE MILE

A pilgrimage through the historic heart of London

Nowhere in London is as densely packed with quirky history, megabucks commerce, grandiose architecture and corners of cultural intrigue as the Square Mile: the traditional heart of the city, and the site of the original Roman settlement of Londinium. From buried temples to future-facing steel towers, this winding ramble takes in the lot.

From Chancery Lane Tube, head towards Holborn, turning left down Chancery Lane itself, passing Lincoln's Inn ❶ on your right and the monumental neo-Gothic Maughan Library ❷ on your left. Once you hit Fleet Street, you have two options. On weekdays, head down Middle Temple Lane, exploring the unusual round structure of Temple Church ❸ – a 12th-century gem built for the Knights Templar, an order of Catholic Crusader soldiers founded to protect medieval pilgrims to Jerusalem. Decompress in the green refuge of Inner Temple Gardens ❹, part

Length: 5km
Walking time without stops: 1 hour
Start: ⊖ Chancery Lane
End: ⊖ Monument

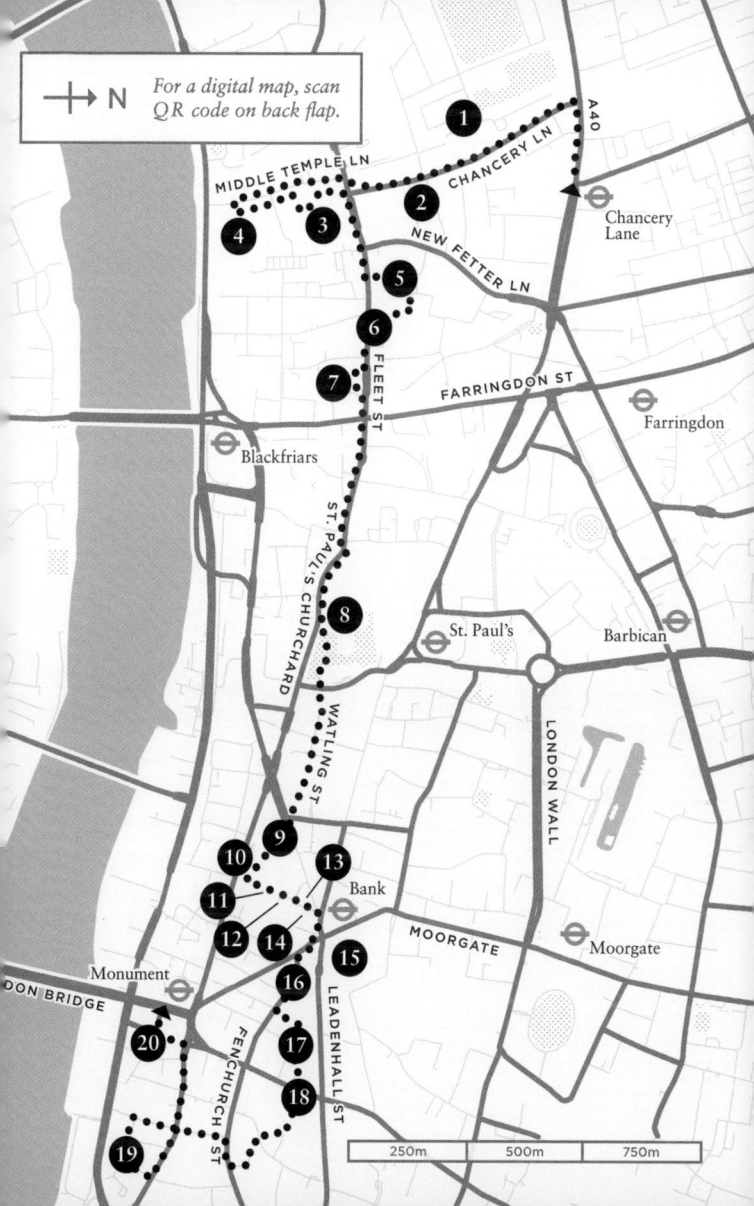

N

MIDDLE TEMPLE LN

CHANCERY LN

A40

Chancery Lane

NEW FETTER LN

FARRINGDON ST

Farringdon

FLEET ST

Blackfriars

ST. PAUL'S CHURCHARD

WATLING ST

St. Paul's

Barbican

LONDON WALL

MOORGATE

Moorgate

Bank

Monument

LEADENHALL ST

FENCHURCH ST

DON BRIDGE

250m 500m 750m

of a working barristers' chambers, only open from 12.30–3pm on weekdays. Then retrace your steps to the main road and continue as follows.

Weekend ramblers should turn left once they hit Fleet Street, before ducking into the lilliputian Johnson's Court. Wind your way to the house museum of esteemed Georgian diarist and inventor of the dictionary, Samuel Johnson **5** (ticketed, should you want to poke around inside). Outside is a darling bronze dedication to his cat, Hodge. Cross Hind Court to Wine Office Court and into Ye Olde Cheshire Cheese **6**. This labyrinthine, hearth-lit pub was reconstructed in 1667 after the Great Fire and patronised by Dickens, Johnson and legions of thirsty hacks from Fleet Street's journalistic heyday in the centuries since.

Stumbling back into daylight, continue east along Fleet Street – thronging with workers from Monday to Friday but remarkably zen on weekends. Turn right down St Bride's Avenue to St Bride's Church **7**, designed by Sir Christopher Wren and boasting his second tallest spire after St Paul's.

Follow the Avenue, and then Bride's Lane, turning east past City Thameslink and approaching St Paul's along Ludgate Hill. What to say about Wren's timeless masterpiece **8**? The English Baroque totem is unsurpassed in the world of ecclesiastical architecture. You could spend an afternoon traipsing its aisles and galleries (it's also worth sticking around for one of its daily evensong services – a free, un-ticketed

Samuel Johnson's House ⑤
Opposite: Temple Church ③

programme of ethereal choral singing that takes place inside the cathedral).

Continue east through the cathedral gardens – festooned with rose bushes and white wisteria – before crossing to the right of the sheeny modern arcade of One New Change (a complex of boutiques and restaurants). Head straight down Watling Street, cross Queen Victoria Street and stop for lunch within the glossy concrete avenue of Bloomberg Arcade ❾: city-best smash-burger chain Bleecker and Japanese udon house Koya are particularly swell.

Turn left at the eldritch 'Forgotten Streams' art installation ❿ commemorating the subterranean channels of the River Walbrook. Under Bloomberg SPACE lies another treasure: the London Mithraeum ⓫. This excavated Roman temple, dedicated to the god Mithras, is one of the city's most haunting archaeological sites. Moments further on is the church of St Stephen Walbrook ⓬ – another Wren classic, with a Byzantine-style array of arches.

Behind the church is a sky-blue decommissioned police phone box; continue past this, with the City of London Magistrates' Court ⓭ on your left and Mansion House ⓮, official home of the Lord Mayor of London, on your right. When you reach Poultry, turn right towards Bank station, taking in the neoclassical colonnades of the Bank of England ⓯ before swerving right and entering Lombard Street ⓰. The street used to be crowded with over 100 cartoonishly

oversized pictorial signs advertising goldsmiths and family-run banks. The few remaining (Victorian facsimiles of the originals) include a cricket, a cat playing a fiddle and a tousled Charles I.

Take the first left up Birchin Lane, ducking right into the narrow walkway of Castle Court. Here you'll find the archaic George & Vulture chophouse **17** – a favourite haunt of Dickens, who mentions it at least 20 times in *The Pickwick Papers*. Continue onwards, skirting the rear garden of St Michael's Cornhill. Exit onto the thrumming thoroughfare of Gracechurch Street and cross into Leadenhall Market **18** – one of the oldest markets in London. Wandering the radial layout of the market, turn right at the dystopian steel Lloyds Building, across Lime Street and down Cullum Street until you hit Fenchurch Street.

At the main road, turn right and left down Rood Lane. Take the second left onto St Dunstan's Lane, leading to the magical gardens of St Dunstan in the East **19**. Ruined during the Blitz, it's now an unexpected sanctuary, the old church walls dotted with trailing plants and incongruous palms. Exit the garden to the northeast, walk north on St Dunstan's Hill and west along Eastcheap, finishing at the Monument to the Great Fire **20**, commemorating the blaze of 1666. Monument station is opposite.

Leadenhall Market **18**

CLERKENWELL
AND BEYOND

Lost rivers, fabulous food and awesome architecture

Historically home to some of the city's most infamous slums, Clerkenwell, Farringdon and their fringes are now among London's most esteemed cultural quarters. From design districts to astounding post-war builds, this tour takes in a wealth of the area's attractions.

Exit Angel station and turn left. Cross the junction to St John Street, turning right at Turner & George butchers ❶ (with its archaic tiled exterior), then left down Arlington Way. Continue to Rosebery Avenue. Immediately on your left is Sadler's Wells ❷, a centre for contemporary dance. This is the sixth theatre to have been built on this site since the late 17th century (this iteration was constructed in 1998). One of its early forebears staged ersatz sea battles in huge water tanks; these days you're more likely to see superlative flamenco and ballet.

Length: 4.6km
Walking time without stops: 1 hour
Start: ⊖ Angel
End: ⊖ Barbican

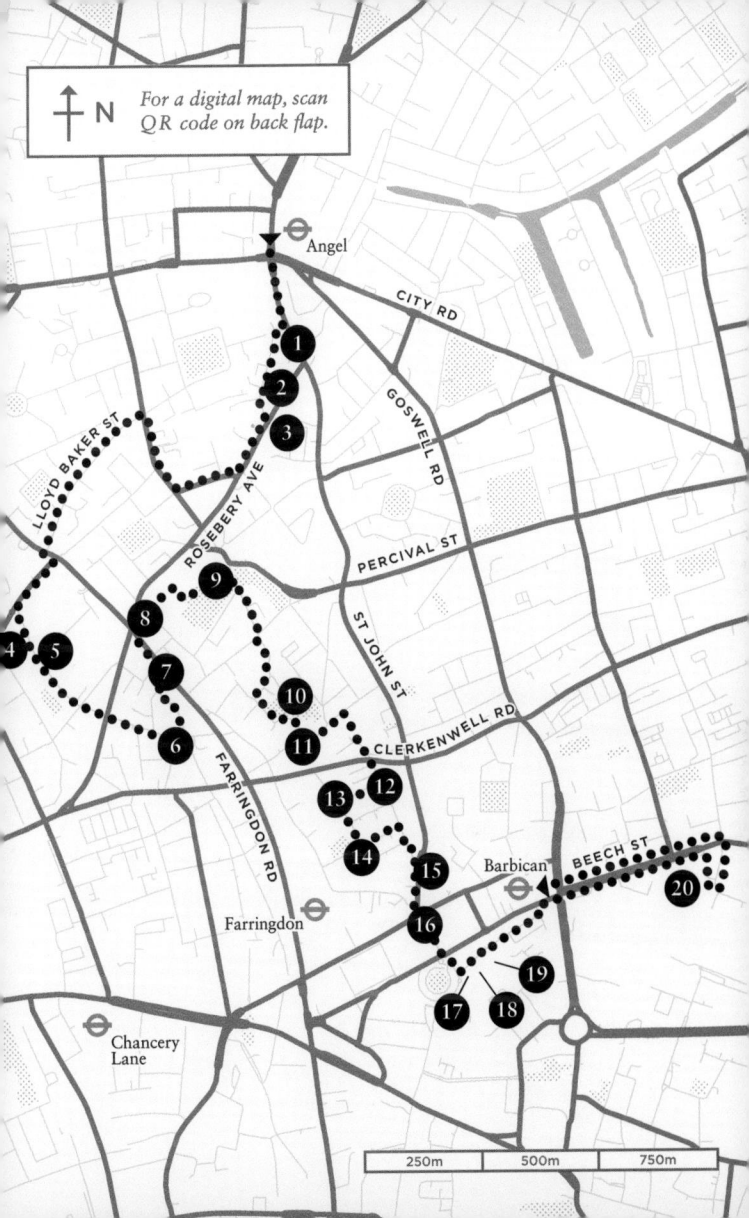

Cross the road. Ahead is Spa Green ❸: an estate built in the 1940s by the modernist architect Berthold Lubetkin and a definitive example of post-war residential design. Turn right, passing Spa Green Gardens on your left, before crossing again and heading up Hardwick Street. Turn right up Amwell Street then left at Lloyd Baker Street and onto the junction at King's Cross Road, crossing over.

Continue on, turning left at Phoenix Place. The Postal Museum ❹ is on your right, and the Mail Rail ❺ on your left. This underground network, formerly used to transfer parcels around the city, is now a fantastic visitor attraction. Cross Mount Pleasant and head under the bridge. You're now in what was once Hockley-in-the-Hole, a former slum, den of iniquity and centre for bear- and bull-baiting in the 17th–18th centuries. Continue to the Coach pub ❻ – a historic landlord was reportedly killed by one of those bears. Peek into the drain grate by the main door to hear the rushing waters of the old River Fleet, which runs beneath your feet here.

Turn left up Crawford Passage until you reach Baker's Row, turning right. On the corner of Farringdon Road is the Eagle ❼: opened in 1991, this was London's very first gastropub and remains a blinding lunch option.

Head left towards the junction with Rosebery Avenue. Cross at the lights and walk along Exmouth Market ❽, lined with bars, pubs and restaurants.

St James Clerkenwell 10

Exmouth Market **1**

Turn right down the dinky passageway to the left of the Church of Our Most Holy Redeemer, entering the grassy oasis of Spa Fields ❾. Cross the park and exit onto Northampton Road, following this street until it becomes Clerkenwell Close. Continue on as the street loops right, past the lofty tower of St James Clerkenwell ❿.

You're now on Clerkenwell Green. To your right is Scotti's Snack Bar ⓫: an Italian-ish caff with a famous chicken escalope sandwich. Stop in if you like, but otherwise turn left, heading along Aylesbury Street and turning right down Jerusalem Passage, crossing St John's Square and Clerkenwell Road.

Head right just before you reach the threshold of St John's Gate ⓬ – built in 1504 as an entry to the headquarters of the Knights of the Order of St John, a band of Catholic crusaders. The cobbled street turns into an alley ending at Britton Street, with the Holy Tavern ⓭ on your left. Housed in a Georgian building – with some original panelling intact – this tiny, candlelit boozer is a perfect pit stop on a wintry day. From here, walk towards the junction with Albion Place, the second left. The modernist building on the corner ⓮, with its geometric grilles and full-size tree on the roof, was built for Janet Street Porter in 1988.

Continue down Albion Place and right onto St John's Lane. At the junction with St John Street, you'll see the white facade of St John ⓯ across the road. Fergus Henderson and Trevor Gulliver's

St John's Gate 12

pioneering, offal-focused restaurant opened in 1994 and remains one of London's essential foodie pilgrimages. It's best to book in advance, though tables in the bar are first come, first served.

Continue south, crossing Charterhouse Street to the Grand Avenue running through the centre of Smithfield meat market **16** – a continuous site of commerce since the medieval era (sadly set to close in 2028). Cross onto West Smithfield and turn left on Cloth Fair. This historic street was once a hub for the medieval fabric trade, former home of poet Sir John Betjeman (look out for his blue plaque) **17** and still the site of London's oldest house (at 41–42, built between 1597–1614) **18** and its oldest parish church, St Bartholomew the Great (founded in 1123) **19**.

Continue as Cloth Fair turns into Middle Street, then turn left onto Cloth Street and right onto Long Lane, crossing the intersection and heading into the tunnel ahead. You're now arriving at the Barbican Estate **20**: lauded cultural centre, sprawling Brutalist icon, aspirational living for the design-savvy and the final stop on our walk. It's worth exploring its splendid galleries, library, tropical conservatory and water gardens. Retracing your steps to Aldersgate Street will find Barbican Tube and your onward transport.

Above: St John **15**
Below: Smithfield Market **16**

3

BOHEMIAN SOHO

Legendary pubs and art-world hangouts

Soho's reputation for bleary-eyed, booze-soaked horny decadence across the latter half of the 20th century wasn't earned by accident. This short tour takes in the district's many classic pubs, nocturnal clubs, extraordinary characters and exhaustingly free-spirited history. Just make sure to stay hydrated…

Exit Tottenham Court Road station onto Charing Cross road. Turn right at Soho Place and cross Soho Square ❶. The surreal Tudor gardener's hut is ersatz, actually an access point for the electricity substation beneath it. Turn down Greek Street. On your left, at number 7, is the former Pillars of Hercules pub ❷ – it's now a ropey Simmons cocktail bar, but for decades was a hangout for London's literary dons, boasting Martin Amis and Ian McEwan as regulars. Across the road, behind an innocuous door at 57, is Trisha's ❸, a subterranean members' club and bastion of the social melting pot that is Soho's after-hours boozing scene.

Length: 1.8km
Walking time without stops: 20 mins
Start: ⊖ *Tottenham Court Road*
End: ⊖ *Piccadilly Circus*

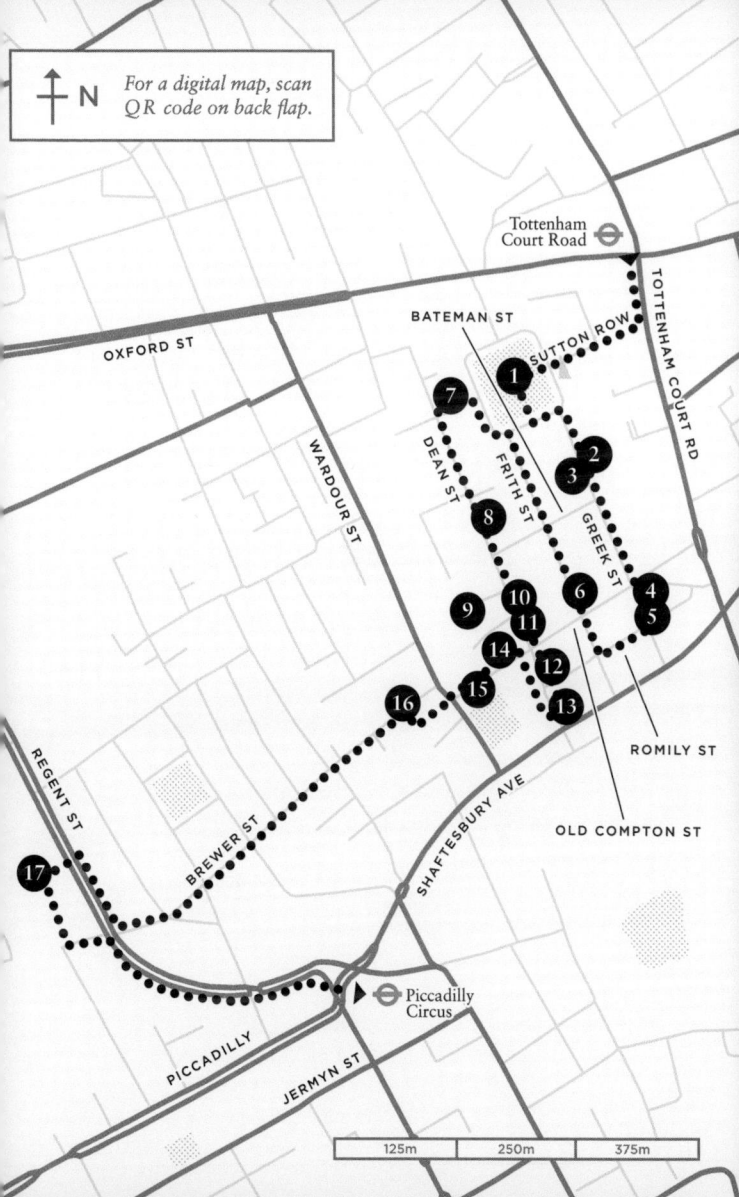

Tottenham
Court Road

BATEMAN ST

SUTTON ROW

OXFORD ST

TOTTENHAM COURT RD

1

7

2

3

DEAN ST

FRITH ST

GREEK ST

8

10

6

4

9

5

11

14

12

15

13

16

ROMILY ST

OLD COMPTON ST

REGENT ST

SHAFTESBURY AVE

BREWER ST

17

PICCADILLY

Piccadilly
Circus

JERMYN ST

125m   250m   375m

Head south and cross Old Compton Street – the inimitable Breton-striped awning of Maison Bertaux ❹ on your left heralds one of London's oldest, and most beloved, patisseries. Next door sits the Coach & Horses ❺. Most famous for its ex-publican, the irascible Norman Balon (known as London's rudest landlord), the Coach was one of the 'Lethal Triangle' of 20th-century Soho drinking dens (along with the Colony Room Club and the French House).

Turn right down Romilly Street and right up Frith Street, passing the unmistakable neon-green sign of Bar Italia ❻ – a long-standing, late-night cafe immortalised by Pulp in their song of the same name. Back at Soho Square, head left on Carlisle Street, past the Guinness-hawking Toucan pub ❼ – the vintage aesthetic of which belies the fact it only opened in 1994 – before turning left onto Dean Street.

Spot the blue plaque to Karl Marx ❽ (palpably *not* a decadent man) above fab modern British restaurant Quo Vadis, before detouring to 7 Meard Street ❾. This was the home of provocative artist and self-styled Soho mega-dandy Sebastian Horsley, once denied US entry for moral turpitude and whose 2010 funeral drew 400 mourners.

Head back towards Dean Street. The space above the restaurant Ducksoup at number 41 was, from 1948–2008, the Colony Room Club ❿ – an infamous and autocratic bar founded by Muriel Belcher and

frequented by Francis Bacon, Lucien Freud, Jeffrey Bernard, Tom Baker, jazz singer George Melly, photographer John Deakin, constituents of the Young British Artists group (YBAs) and innumerable other members of Soho's bohemian and alcoholic classes over the decades.

A few doors down lies the members-only Groucho Club ⓫ – a '90s institution, also beloved of the YBAs and Britpop crowd – now operated by gallery behemoth Hauser & Wirth. Just across Old Compton Street is the French House ⓬ – still Soho's best pub, populated by literary deviants (despite only serving half pints). The upstairs dining room, with its robust menu of calf brains in brown butter, roast magret duck and profiteroles, might be London's finest restaurant (and a perfect place to stop for food – advance booking essential).

Continue south. At number 52 is Gerry's Club ⓭, another stalwart of Soho's grimy glory days, fuelled by cheap wine and louche jazz (and also technically a members' club, albeit one with a slack entry policy, if one fancies smooth-talking the doorman...).

From here, retrace your steps and turn left down Old Compton Street, the heart of queer London, past the classic gay pubs of the Admiral Duncan ⓮ and Comptons ⓯. This is where Dylan Thomas is said to have accidentally left his first manuscript of *Under Milk Wood* when legless, back when it was called the Swiss Tavern.

Soho Square ❶

Traipse down Tisbury Court, turning right on Rupert Street to gawp at the eye-popping signage of the old Raymond Revue Bar **16**. The strip club and adult theatre is long gone, but the neon sign advertising itself as an 'international striptease spectacular' remains. Turn left down Brewer Street, continue along Glasshouse Street, turn right at Regent Street and finally left onto Heddon Street, to Australian all-day restaurant Ziggy Green **17**. No, we're not ending with an anticlimactic brunch: rather, hit the basement, where artists Darren Coffield and Justin Hibbs have co-created a wonderfully faithful facsimile of the Colony Room Club, replete with original artwork, racing-green walls, 2008 bar prices and, supposedly, some of the same punters. It's a sweet homage to a glorious (if utterly debauched) era we're unlikely to see anew.

Retrace your steps to Regent Street and turn right to find your end destination of Piccadilly Circus Tube.

LITERARY BLOOMSBURY

In the footsteps of great writers

The cosmopolitan central London neighbourhood of Bloomsbury brims with bookish history – this tour takes in its highbrow highlights.

Exit the station onto St Pancras Road and head towards the intersection with Euston Road. Turn right, passing the St Pancras Renaissance London Hotel ❶, designed by George Gilbert Scott in the Gothic Revival style. Cross Midland Road. On your right is the British Library ❷: a red-brick behemoth, its forecourt dominated by Eduardo Paolozzi's enormous bronze sculpture of Isaac Newton. You'll need a pass to use the reading rooms, but there is a slew of public shops, cafes and galleries (the Treasures collection includes the Magna Carta and Domesday Book).

Exit onto Euston Road and cross over, turning left at the Pret onto Mabledon Place. Head south, past the tennis courts on your right and a plaque to Sir Rowland Hill ❸, pioneer of the postal service, on your

Length: 6km
Walking time without stops: 1 hour 15 mins
Start: ⊖ King's Cross St Pancras
End: ⊖ King's Cross St Pancras

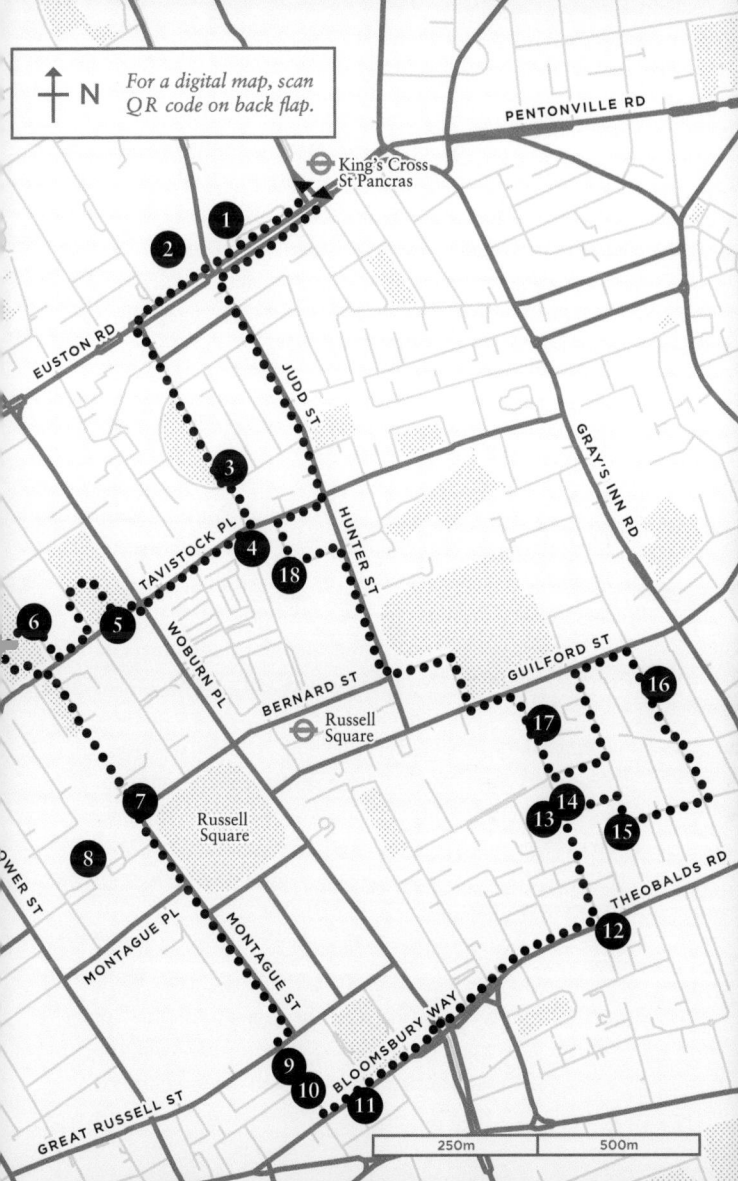

N

PENTONVILLE RD

King's Cross
St Pancras

1

2

EUSTON RD

JUDD ST

GRAY'S INN RD

3

HUNTER ST

4

18

TAVISTOCK PL

WOBURN PL

6

5

GUILFORD ST

16

BERNARD ST

Russell
Square

17

7

Russell
Square

13 14

15

8

THEOBALDS RD

MONTAGUE PL

MONTAGUE ST

12

OWER ST

BLOOMSBURY WAY

9

10

GREAT RUSSELL ST

11

250m   500m

left, until you reach the intersection of Marchmont Street and Tavistock Place. Turn right, but note Gay's the Word ❹, London's preeminent queer bookshop – and the UK's oldest, established in 1979 – just ahead.

Head west along Tavistock Place, crossing at Woburn Place onto Tavistock Square. On your left is the Tavistock Hotel ❺; a small blue plaque to the left of the entrance commemorates modernist writers and Bloomsbury Group mainstays Virginia and Leonard Woolf, who lived at a house on this site from 1924–39.

Walk through the park and exit on the west side; head left, turning right on Gordon Square. Walk along the edge of the park, past more tightly packed Bloomsbury Group plaques ❻: to critic and biographer Lytton Strachey (at 51); art critic Clive Bell (at 50); and painters Vanessa Bell and Duncan Grant, and economist John Maynard Keynes (all at 46). It was here that the Bloomsbury Group formed via gatherings hosted by sisters Virginia and Vanessa, who lived at number 46 in the early 1900s; their unconventional and cross-pollinating relationships were best summed up by the American writer and celebrated wit, Dorothy Parker: 'They lived in squares, painted in circles and loved in triangles.'

Enter the park's eastern entrance, turn left across its pleasant lawns and exit next to the kiosk. Walk down Woburn Square, past the concrete edifice of SOAS University of London. When you reach the corner of Russell Square, note number 24 to your left:

from 1929–71, this was the offices of publisher Faber & Faber **❼** (there's a bonus brown plaque commemorating poet and playwright TS Eliot – who worked for the imprint from 1925 until his death in 1965 – on the building's Thornhaugh Street vestibule).

Turn around and head back to the corner of the square. The towering white pile ahead of you is Senate House **❽**, an Art Deco icon and University of London library complex. The building was repurposed by the government for use as Ministry of Information offices during WWII and George Orwell, who worked there, is said to have used it as inspiration for *1984*'s imposing Ministry of Truth.

Continue south onto Montague Street. Turn right onto Great Russell Street and left onto Bury Place, past the wonderful London Review Bookshop **❾** and stationers Present & Correct **❿**. Turn left onto Bloomsbury Way. Across the road at 20–21 is Swedenborg House **⓫**: bookshop and HQ of the Swedenborg Society, dedicated to the titular 18th-century philosopher, writer and scientist.

Cross Southampton Row onto Theobalds Road and walk until you reach Lamb's Conduit Street. Lunch options abound. You could pay a visit to city-best chippy The Fryer's Delight **⓬**, a few paces onwards on the opposite side of the road. Or you can turn left down Lamb's Conduit for fancier options, including wine-focused bistro Noble Rot **⓭** and airy Levantine staple Honey & Co **⓮**.

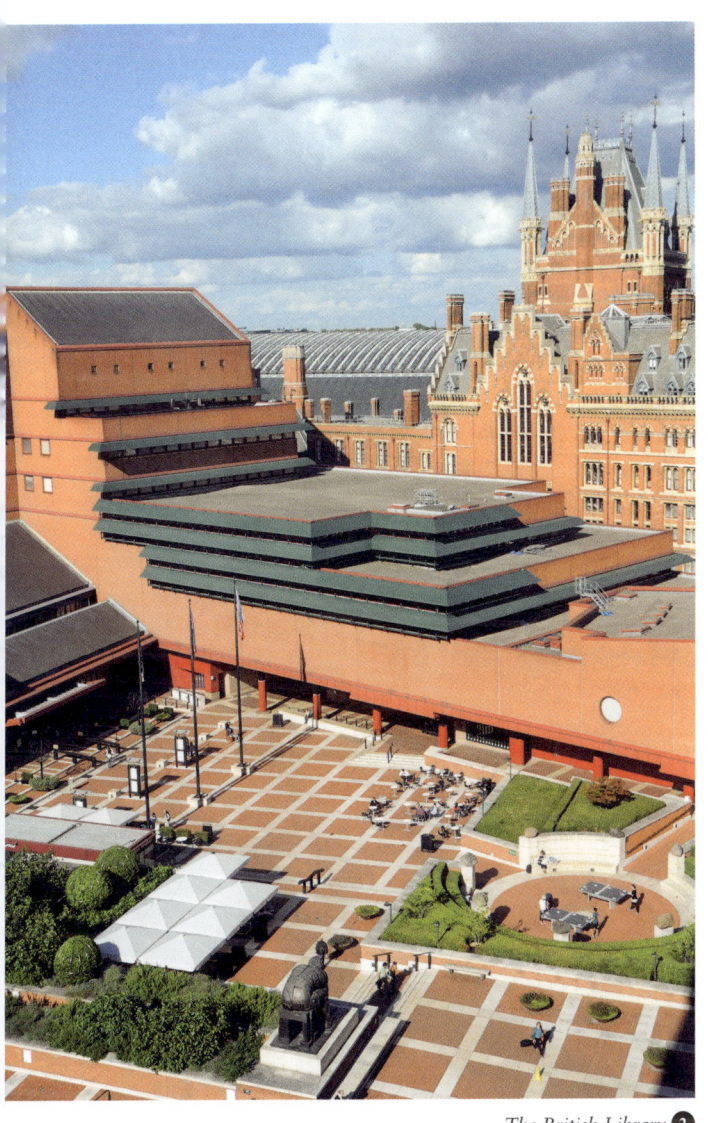

The British Library ❷

Turn right on Rugby Street, then right again between the Rugby Tavern and a red-tiled housing block, noting a plaque to crime novelist and playwright Dorothy L Sayers **15** to the left of the pub. Turn left onto Northington Street, then left again onto John Street. Continue as it becomes Doughty Street – around half way up, at number 48, is the Charles Dickens Museum **16**, occupying an address he lived at from 1837–39. His time here may have been brief, but the museum has a mighty collection of over 1,000 objects of Dickens paraphernalia.

Turn left on Guilford Street, left on Millman Street, right on Great Ormond Street and right again to emerge back on Lamb's Conduit Street. It's worth stopping at the Lamb pub **17**: a beatific, wood-panelled boozer supposedly frequented by Dickens (and later by Sylvia Plath and Ted Hughes).

Thirst quenched, head north and rejoin Guilford Street, turning left and then right on Lansdowne Terrace. Skirt Brunswick Square Gardens, continuing down Hunter Street, then left at Handel Street to reach the final stop of your literary pilgrimage: Skoob **18** – a cracking second-hand bookshop. Done browsing, make your way back to King's Cross St Pancras by turning right on Kenton Street, right again on Tavistock Place, then left on Judd Street. Head north until you hit Euston Road, with St Pancras station to your right.

EAST LONDON THROUGH THE AGES

Huguenots to hipsters (via baddies, bells and beigels)

East London may be the city's evergreen hipster stomping ground, but it's also a place of incredible diversity. From the French Huguenots who arrived in London in the 1700s, to later waves of Jewish and Bengali immigration – especially around Brick Lane – the panoply of cultures is a fundamental part of the district's character (though its morbid associations with Jack the Ripper and the Krays remain a draw). This centuries-spanning stroll takes in the lot.

Turn left from the station: 150 m or so on the same side of the road is the Blind Beggar pub ❶. Now a homogenous boozer, it was enshrined in East End lore on 9 March 1966 as the place Ronnie Kray shot rival gangster George Cornell.

Retrace your steps, turning right up Brady Street, then left on Durward Street. The sheeny facade of

Length: 6.8km

Walking time without stops: 1 hour 25 mins

Start: ✪ Whitechapel

End: ✪ London Fields

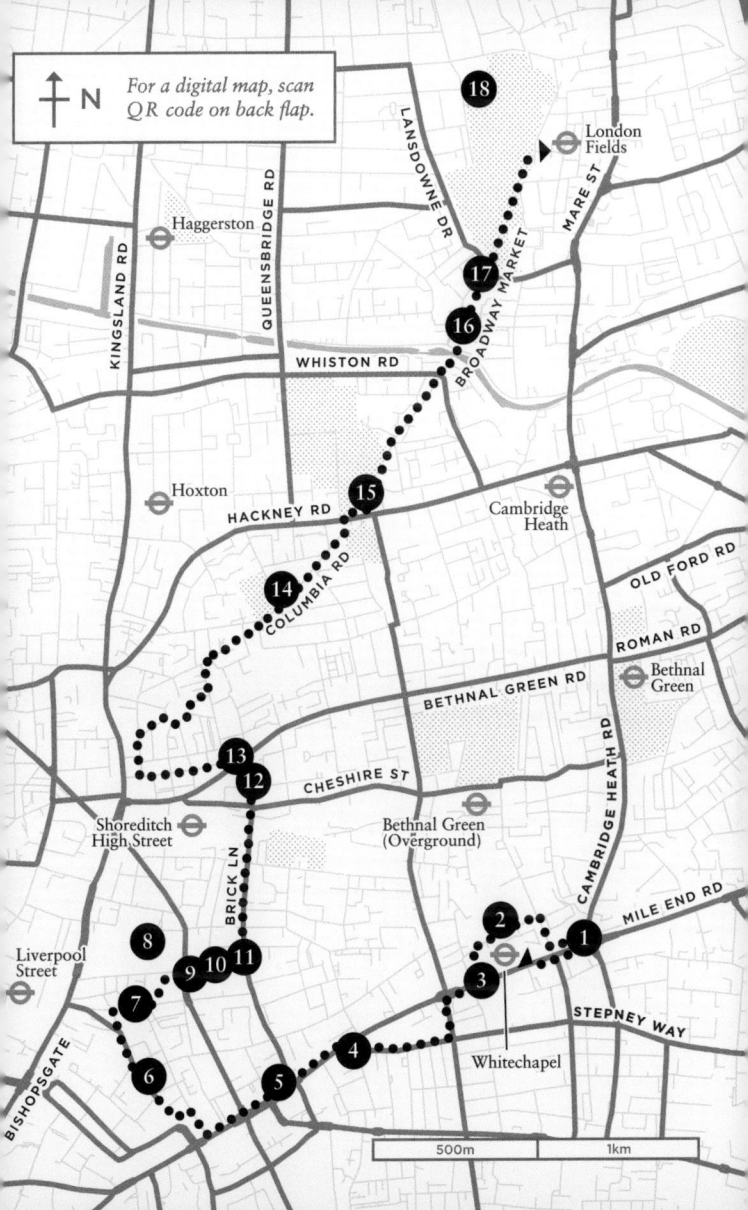

the station's modern back entrance may look innocuous, but it was here that Jack the Ripper left his first victim, Mary Ann Nichols, back when it was a dowdy backstreet stables in 1888 ❷. Continue on, past a wildflower bank, turning left on the pedestrianised Court Street. When you reach the main road, look down. You'll be standing near the Whitechapel Fatberg Memorial Manhole Cover ❸, commemorating the removal of the 250m-long, congealed mass of bathroom detritus found in the sewers below in 2017.

Cross the road and turn right. Pass the Royal London Hospital then turn left on New Road. Turn right on Fieldgate Street and walk on until the T-junction. A weathered sign opposite heralds the Whitechapel Bell Foundry ❹, who fashioned enormous church bells (including the Liberty Bell, a famous symbol of American freedom) for 450 years, until it shuttered in 2017. Turn left on Whitechapel Road. Cross after the park, continuing west. You could stop here to visit the Whitechapel Gallery ❺ – designed in the Art Nouveau 'British modern' style – or plough on, crossing the junction next to Aldgate East Tube.

Turn right on Goulston Street, then left over an unmarked, tree-lined cut-through, before turning right on Middlesex Street. Continue, passing Wentworth Street on your right. From Sunday to Friday, this is where you'll find the stalls of Petticoat Lane Market ❻, a hub for selling clothes, and later Huguenot garment manufacturing, from the 1600s on.

Continue straight, turning right on Sandy's Row, and right again on Artillery Passage, continuing into Artillery Lane to reach Raven Row ❼. This arts hub shows multidisciplinary works in an 18th-century building affixed with two shiny galleries. Cross Crispin Street, turning left through the London Fruit and Wool Exchange building to reach Brushfield Street, an entrance to Spitalfields Market ❽ (an emporium of street food, clothes, homeware and more). You could stop here for lunch, but it's worth holding out for a famous Brick Lane beigel just a few streets away.

Turn right towards Christ Church Spitalfields ❾, designed by Nicholas Hawksmoor and consecrated in 1729. Cross to Fournier Street ❿. Many of the beautiful terraced Georgian houses here were once home to émigré Huguenot silk weavers (the hand-shaped door knockers on several houses are a Huguenot motif). More recently, artist duo Gilbert & George moved into number 8 in 1968 and have been there since.

Continue straight, turning left at Brick Lane; the mosque on the corner ⓫ is housed in what was once a Huguenot church. Head north, past the umpteen curry houses. Sometimes known as 'Bangla Town', this street and its surrounds have been home to a large Bangladeshi diaspora since the 1950s–70s. At the other end of Brick Lane you'll find the beigel shops, a reminder of the area's earlier history as a haven for Jews escaping Eastern European pogroms in the 19–20th centuries. For time immemorial (well, since 1974), Beigel Shop ⓬

and Beigel Bake **13** have fought a benign war over who's hawking the better chewy Jewish breads. Either way, a salt beef beigel slicked with sinus-ripping mustard and pickles is a fine lunch indeed.

Continue north, crossing Bethnal Green Road slightly left to Redchurch Street, with its smattering of chic shops. Turn right on Boundary Street and right again on Navarre Street. At Arnold Circus, follow the circular gardens (centrepoint of the Boundary Estate, the world's oldest social housing project) and turn right on Palissy Street, then wind your way eastwards towards Columbia Road **14**: a delightful parade of restaurants, bakeries, record shops, domestic boutiques and, on Sundays, an iconic flower market.

Continue east, turning left as the road ends. Cross Hackney Road and turn right, then left up Goldsmiths Row, past Hackney City Farm **15**. Head straight, over the canal, towards Broadway Market. This bustling mass of cafes, pubs and bookshops (Artwords **16** and the esoteric Donlon Books **17** are particularly fab), plus a weekend market, is populated by well-dressed Hackney families and their better-dressed dogs.

At the market's top end, cross the road to enter London Fields, home to the Olympic-sized London Fields Lido **18**. Follow a path diagonally northeast. Exit at Martello Street and turn right, then left on Martello Terrace to find London Fields Overground.

Clockwise from top left: Fournier Street 10;
Beigel Bake 13; *Broadway Market; Beigel Bake* 13.

THE LINE ART TRAIL

Public sculpture walk through east London

Launched in 2015, the curated art walk of The Line is a fine way to take in the industrial edgelands of east and south London, dotted with thought-provoking contemporary works from a host of esteemed artists (with a couple of easy linking sections via rail and cable).

From the station barriers, turn right and right again after exiting. The quickest route to the start of the walk is through Westfield shopping centre, following signs for Queen Elizabeth Olympic Park. Ascend the steps in front of you and pass straight through. Turn left on the glass-covered walkway, before the Big Easy BBQ restaurant, then right on the main artery of shops and restaurants – you'll see the lofty roof of the London Stadium in the near distance.

Head straight on. Just ahead, Anish Kapoor's *ArcelorMittal Orbit* tower ❶ rises towards the clouds. This mess of latticed red steel, curling around a central tower containing elevators and stairs to an observation

Length: 7.5km
Walking time without stops: 1 hour 30 mins
Start: ⬦ Stratford International
End: ⬦ North Greenwich

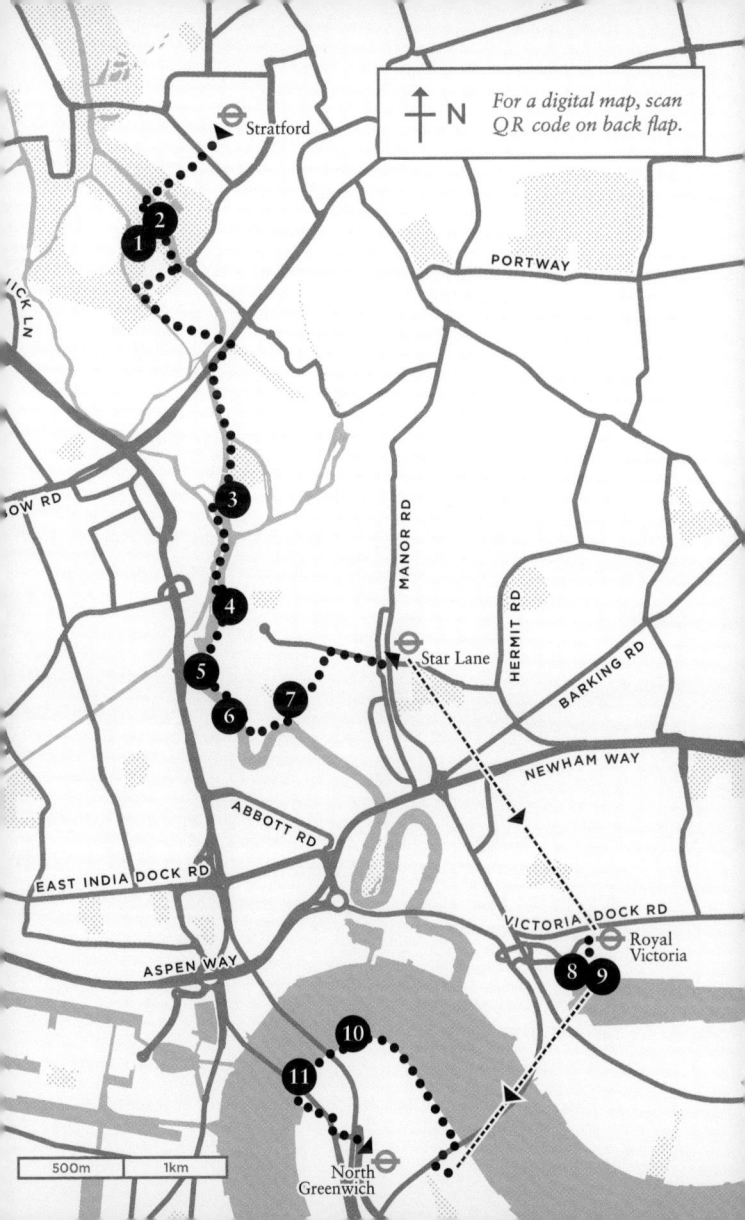

N

For a digital map, scan QR code on back flap.

Stratford

PORTWAY

1CK LN

OW RD

MANOR RD

HERMIT RD

BARKING RD

Star Lane

NEWHAM WAY

ABBOTT RD

EAST INDIA DOCK RD

VICTORIA DOCK RD

ASPEN WAY

Royal Victoria

North Greenwich

500m   1km

deck – all inspired by the Tower of Babel – is as divisive now as it was when it opened in 2012. But it's undeniably striking, and the tube slide that runs from the top of it is a zippy embellishment by German artist Carsten Höller.

After crossing the WaterWorks River, immediately turn left down the steps to the waterfront, and then right to proceed with the water on your left. From here until the end of the walk, the route is clearly demarcated with red and blue stickers at regular intervals.

After a minute's walk, set back from the water's edge, is Mahtab Hussain's *Please Take a Seat* ❷. This riff on a Victorian park bench includes sculpted motifs of things associated with Newham borough, from the Bow Bells to a microphone held by a disembodied grime MC (as well as portraits of the local Youth Collective with whom Hussain conceived the bench).

Continue along the water. At the time of writing, the path was undergoing works, so turn right at the blue iron bridge, ascending the ramped path and heading west across a stretch of open ground to the left of the monumental slatted-concrete edifice of UCL East. (Or, if the path remains open, continue south along this waterway and cross at the High Street to rejoin the route at the Three Mills Wall River Weir.)

Descend the bank to the water's edge (now the City Mill River) and turn left. At High Street, cross and turn right, proceeding until you reach the river again. Turn left to rejoin the river path. Heading

Anish Kapoor's ArcelorMittal Orbit tower ❶

south, you'll soon pass peaceful Three Mills marina. Historic Three Mills Island ❸ is just ahead, the conical white oast roofs of Clock Mill visible above the rooftops. Turn right onto the cobbles of Three Mill Lane and then head south on the sliver of land between Bow Creek and the Lea.

Just before the dowdy white footbridge curving off to the Limehouse Cut, take a ramp marked Leaway South to rejoin the road. Turn right – towards the gasometers – and right again down the Leaway steps. Head left, past Eva Rothschild's striped *Living Spring* ❹, a work of 'magic minimalism' evoking a sapling. Continue on, past a lofty vertical assemblage of 22 shopping trolleys by Abigail Fallis ❺; and Helen Cammock's wistful text work *On WindTides* ❻, emblazoned on either side of a bridge over the Lea, reflecting on emotional and geographical transiences.

Follow the creek as it turns to the left, then enter Cody Dock ❼, a sweetly ramshackle, post-industrial regeneration project comprising community gardens, commissioned artworks, a wild rolling footbridge (that can be moved to let ships pass beneath) and a tiny cafe, perfect for restocking on soft drinks or restorative treats. Exit by the cafe and head straight on South Crescent. Turn right on Cody Road, past warehouses, studios and a pizza bar. At the junction, enter Star Lane DLR and jump on a train south to Royal Victoria (just a short two-stop hop towards Beckton, though you may need to change at Canning Town).

Exit Royal Victoria DLR on Seagull Lane and turn right. Cross at the junction, heading towards the water with City Hall on your right. Turn left to reach Yinka Ilori's playfully massive chairs **8**, covered in African diasporic Dutch-wax-print patterns.

Retrace your steps slightly to the station for the IFS Cloud Cable Car **9** – a vertiginous gondola lift over the Thames, and a bargain price (by paper ticket, Oyster or contactless). Ascend and soak up the wonderful panoramic views on the journey over to the Greenwich Peninsula.

Leave the peninsula terminal and head east back to the water. Turn left to follow the Thames around the O2 arena. The home straight factors five works in quick succession, not least Serge Attukwei Clottey's *Tribe and Tribulation* **10** (a reclaimed wood totem embracing themes of the ocean, migration and the reuse of materials, with integrated sound recordings made at former slave forts on the African Gold Coast) and Thomson & Craighead's irreverent *Here* signpost **11** (placed on the prime meridian line, its '24,859 >' text referencing the Earth's full circumference).

Follow Drawdock Road and turn right on Ordnance Crescent. Turn right at Millennium Way and cross near the bike storage – North Greenwich is in front of you.

Tribe and Tribulation, Serge Attukwei Clottey **10**

7

THE LEA RIVER

From Walthamstow Wetlands to Limehouse Basin

London's nicest north–south waterway makes for a fascinating few hours – from the still, barge-lined levels adjoining east London's wetlands to the buzzy historical industry of Bow and the docklands.

Turn left out of the station. Ascend the steps and walk left along Ferry Lane, following a sign for 'Walthamstow Wetlands'. Pass a set of traffic lights and some red railings with views down to the slim waterway of Pymmes Brook, then turn right down a cobbled slope on the right-hand side of the Lea River.

Continue on, past the red-brick estate on your right and the first of many houseboats you'll see. Behind the opposite riverbank – albeit largely hidden behind a wall of trees and aquatic greenery – are the Walthamstow Wetlands ❶, one of the largest urban nature reserves of their kind in Europe, and a stopover for migratory birdlife. Pass Markfield Park, home to the Markfield Beam Engine and Museum ❷, with a

Length: 13.1km
Walking time without stops: 2 hours 40 mins
Start: ⊖ Tottenham Hale
End: ⊖ Limehouse

For a digital map, scan QR code on back flap.

N

Tottenham Hale

FERRY LN

HIGH RD

Clapton

CHATSWORTH RD

HOMERTON RD

Hackney Wick

QUEENSBRIDGE RD

MARE ST

WHISTON RD

HACKNEY RD

ROMAN RD

GROVE RD

BRICK LN

MILE END RD

STEPNEY WAY

COMMERCIAL RD

BOW RD

HIGH ST

Limehouse

1km   2km

Victorian contraption that once pumped sewage from Tottenham to the east London suburbs. Slightly further on is the Lea Rowing Club ❸. Its adjoining cafe is perfect for a quick coffee or artisan ginger beer.

Veer slightly off the river to a parallel track signposted Spring Lane, before crossing the water on a footbridge adjacent to some tennis courts, and turning right to continue following the curve of the river south. This green expanse, with its mix of meadows, reeds and pylons, is Walthamstow Marshes ❹: a semi-natural grassland floodplain, grazed by native breed cattle in the summer and home to over 900 plant and insect species (plus myriad birds, amphibians and reptiles). Continue ahead, traversing a cattle grid, before crossing the river again, over a slim white metal footbridge. Turn left, past new-build apartments and Millfields Park, passing under Lea Bridge and perhaps pausing for a drink at the balmy waterside benches of the Princess of Wales ❺.

As the river forks, continue ahead on what is now the Hackney Cut: an artificial channel created to straighten the Lea's watercourse in 1770 (the left-hand fork through the weir follows the original channel). Cross the footbridge and enter the Middlesex Filter Beds ❻ on your left. Built to purify London's water supply during the cholera outbreak of the mid-1800s, they're now a 10-acre wildlife haven.

Cross the round, covered reservoir, turning right at the next junction and continuing straight as the

Walthamstow Wetlands ❶

cricket and football pitches of Hackney Marshes loom into view, rejoining the river towpath on your right and turning left to continue south. Around 1.4km later, you'll pass below the A12's noisy carriageways: note the sweet, DIY assemblages of painted junk affixed to the columns. Pressing on towards Hackney Wick, you'll hit a footbridge to the left of the huge Hackney Bridge food court. If you fancy a detour, turn left here onto East Bay Lane and right on Parkes Street to the V&A East Storehouse ❼, a multi-level repository for the globe-spanning museum's astounding inventory.

Alternatively, cross the footbridge and follow Wallis Road, turning left past Hackney Wick station and onto White Post Lane, then left again towards the water, where you'll find two lunch options: the stalwart pizza/beer joint Crate ❽, and pioneering zero-waste restaurant Silo ❾ (lunchtime only on Saturdays).

Calories in, cross the river and turn right down the Slipway to rejoin the towpath at the buzzy Barge East bar ❿. The curvaceous roof of the London Stadium will soon appear to your left, with Anish Kapoor's warped helter-skelter sculpture, the *ArcelorMittal Orbit*, peeking up beyond. At the Old Ford Lock ⓫, you rejoin the River Lea proper. The cottages adjacent to the lock were the filming locale for arch '90s telly staple *The Big Breakfast*.

From here, things become rather more urban on the approach to Bow Creek. Cross the river on a wooden-fenced walkway signposted towards Three

Approaching Hackney Wick

Mills Island and Limehouse Basin. Pass under the roaring A118, past decrepit warehouses and new-build flats, before crossing again to Three Mills Island ⑫ opposite a large Tesco. The archaic site of some of Britain's oldest mills, the complex is still home to the resplendent Georgian Clock Mill (with its oast towers and giant timepiece) and Grade I-listed House Mill (the largest tidal mill on earth).

Turn right straight after the footbridge and follow the path along a thin island, past scrubby foliage and gasometers on your left, crossing Bow Locks on a curved, stepped walkway. Continue straight onto a slatted-wooden walkway along a more slender waterway. You're now on the Limehouse Cut; simply follow the water all the way to the pristine marina of the Limehouse Basin itself. On arrival, duck into the Cruising Association ⑬ bar for a celebratory snifter: what it lacks in urbane cache it makes up for in 1980s timewarp vibes, with a lovely aspect of the barges bobbing outside.

From there, cross the narrow bridge across the basin lock, turn right and follow the water to the basin's western edge. Turn right up Branch Road: Limehouse DLR is directly ahead.

AN EPPING FOREST CIRCULAR

Vast expanse of age-old trees and lush grasslands

Explore the city's preeminent ancient woodland via a circular route from the far east London outpost of Chingford, 30 minutes on the train from Liverpool Street. The simple route offers a fine opportunity to truly zone out in deep greenery (even with the ever-present hum of the A104 in the background).

Alighting at Chingford, exit the station and turn right, heading towards the distant treetops. Chingford Plain will soon emerge into view. Cross onto Bury Road and turn right along a broad path just before Chingford Golf Club. Turn slightly right uphill, past a branchless tree with no bark; the path will lead you to the striking white box of Queen Elizabeth's Hunting Lodge ❶, just through a gate guarded by two deer sculptures. Built on the orders of Henry VIII in 1543 and restored by his daughter, it now features a small museum that includes

Length: 10.3km
Walking time without stops: 2 hours
Starts: ⇌ Chingford
Ends: ⇌ Chingford

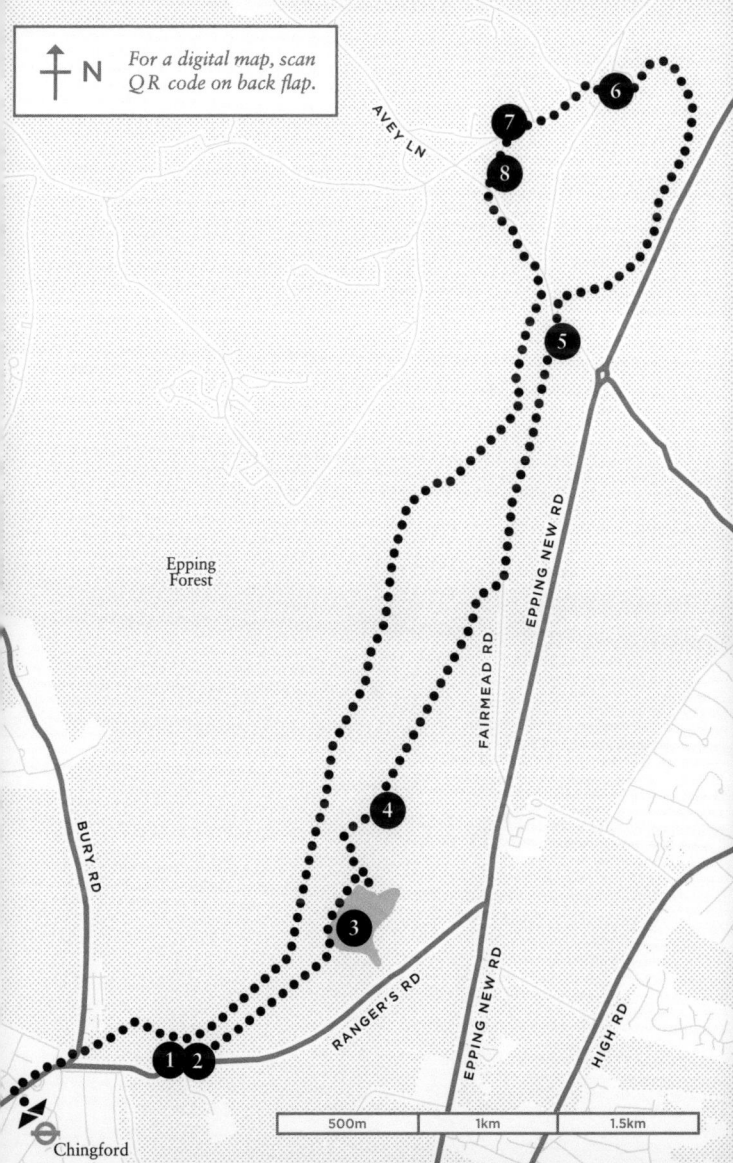

AVEY LN

7

6

8

5

Epping
Forest

EPPING NEW RD

FAIRMEAD RD

4

3

BURY RD

RANGER'S RD

EPPING NEW RD

HIGH RD

1 2

Chingford

500m   1km   1.5km

a dressing-up area and, from the second floor, spectacular views across the forest.

Grab a coffee at the neighbouring Larder – within the white clapboard barn of Butler's Retreat ❷ – or snoop around the Epping Forest visitor centre, before heading back to the path and a route signposted the 'Willow Trail'. This will take you eastwards through scrubland, the route demarcated every so often with carved effigies of characters from children's book series, Brambly Hedge. Keep an eye out for the English Longhorn cattle who have grazed here for centuries and form a key part of the forest's conservation efforts.

After ten minutes or so, the trail crosses over a wider path and you enter the woods, before emerging at Connaught Water ❸. Created by the Corporation of London in the late 1800s out of a local marsh, the eight-acre lake now forms a haven for local wildlife with swans, tufted ducks and grey herons all lining up for townies to take their pictures. As you hit the lake, turn left, walking around a third of the water's edge. A little before you reach a bridge, take a path due north on a rough track next to a bench into the woods (you can tell it's the correct one from the circular, tree-filled divot as the path closes in: the probable remnants of a wartime bomb crater).

After a few minutes in the undergrowth, emerge onto a wide path: turn right and then right again onto the creatively named Main Path. Continue on, taking

a very slight left at the lofty landmark of Grimston's Oak ❹ (named for Victorian cricketer and electric telegraphy pioneer Robert Grimston, who urged clearance of the area around the tree). Walk through mixed woodlands of beech and hornbeam for around a kilometre until you hit the concrete Fairmead Path. Take a left and continue for around 20 minutes until you reach the cash-only Original Tea Hut ❺: an Epping Forest icon, ramshackle and utilitarian but beloved by dog walkers, motorbikers and first-date hikers alike.

With the tea hut on your right, turn left on the minor road for around 30m before turning right back into the woods at Gate 82. You are now back on the Main Path, which will lead you all the way through an undulating track up to High Beach. Looping left at the end of the track – opposite a slightly hidden pond to your right – and emerging from the trees onto a road, you'll be greeted by the hulking Kings Oak pub and hotel ahead, with its adjoining Oyster Shack & Seafood Bar ❻. Once a hidden gem, the shack has undeniably been discovered by Hackney's weekend-rambling masses, but the quality of the Irish oysters, Cornish mackerel and dressed Cromer crabs hasn't been impacted. Settle in with a pint from the neighbouring pub on the benches outside for a welcome break.

Fully rested and watered, cross the road and green directly in front of the Kings Oak, to the road on the far side. Turn left and head back into the forest. Continue

on, watching for traffic but ignoring any junctions to the side until you reach Arabin House **7** on the right (with a red post box set into the wall), where you should take the left fork down Church Lane, leading past the Victorian Gothic Holy Innocents Church **8**. Soon after the church you'll meet a T-junction; cross over the verge and take the path in the woods, turning left and following it parallel to the road. Follow this until you reach a larger, sandier path intersecting horizontally just after a road junction on the left.

Turn right, remaining on the track and ignoring any turns for around 2.5km, relaxing into the tranquil, uniform greenery and enjoying the plentiful beeches, field maples, oaks and hawthorn as you go. You will eventually cross over a small stream back onto Chingford Plain, with the Queen Elizabeth's Hunting Lodge peeking through foliage to your left. From here, you can pick up the original path, returning to the bright lights of Chingford and its station.

9

CRYSTAL PALACE TO NUNHEAD CEMETERY

From dinosaurs to the dead via the Green Chain

The full south London Green Chain is a sprawling, 80km walking route from Thamesmead to Nunhead. This walk is a modified version of its final stretch, tweaked to include awesome panoramic viewpoints, a spooky folly and some truly outré sculpture among the woodland glades and peaceful parkland.

Turn right from the station and into Crystal Palace Park, heading right downhill until you reach Lower Lake and its array of delightfully inaccurate dinosaur statues (plus other ancient megafauna) ❶ standing sentinel over the water. Designed and sculpted by Benjamin Waterhouse Hawkins from 1852–54, they're one of London's most beguiling sights.

After looping the lake, retrace your steps to the station and follow the Green Chain signs north across the park, vaguely in the direction of the gargantuan

Length: 12.2km
Walking time without stops: 2 hours 30 mins
Start: ⊖ Crystal Palace
End: ⇌ Nunhead

Crystal Palace Park dinosaurs ❶

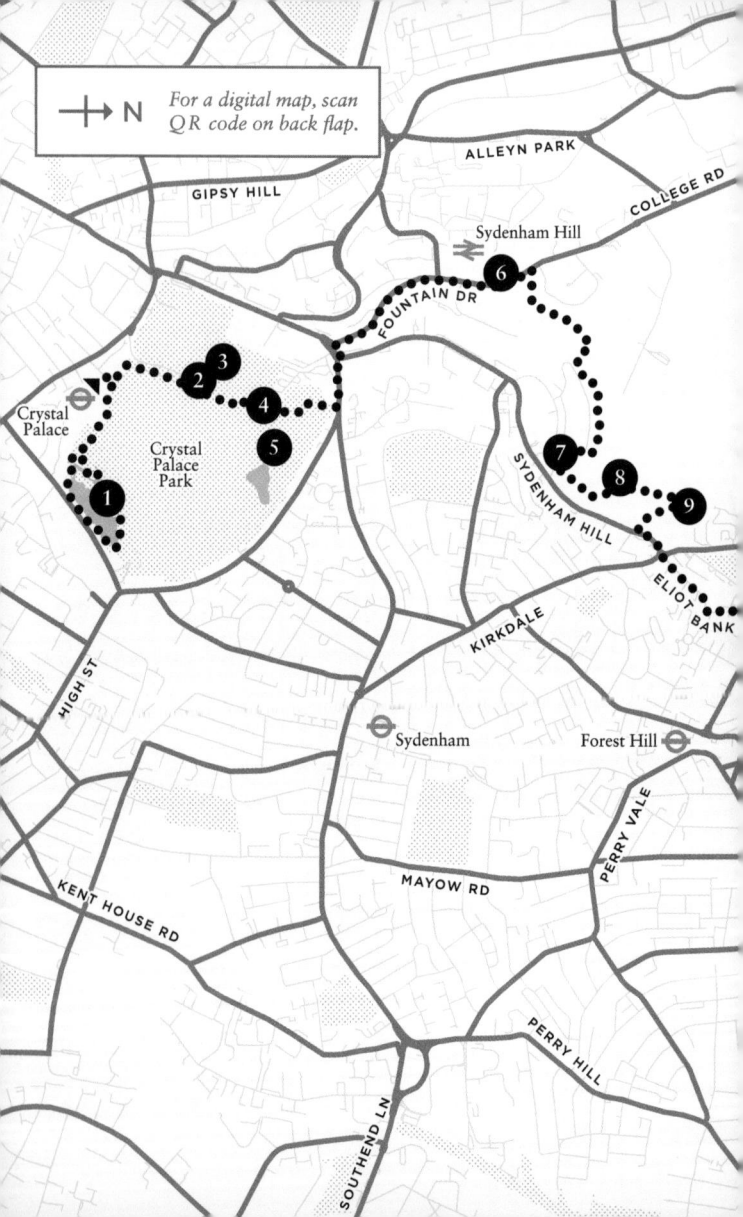

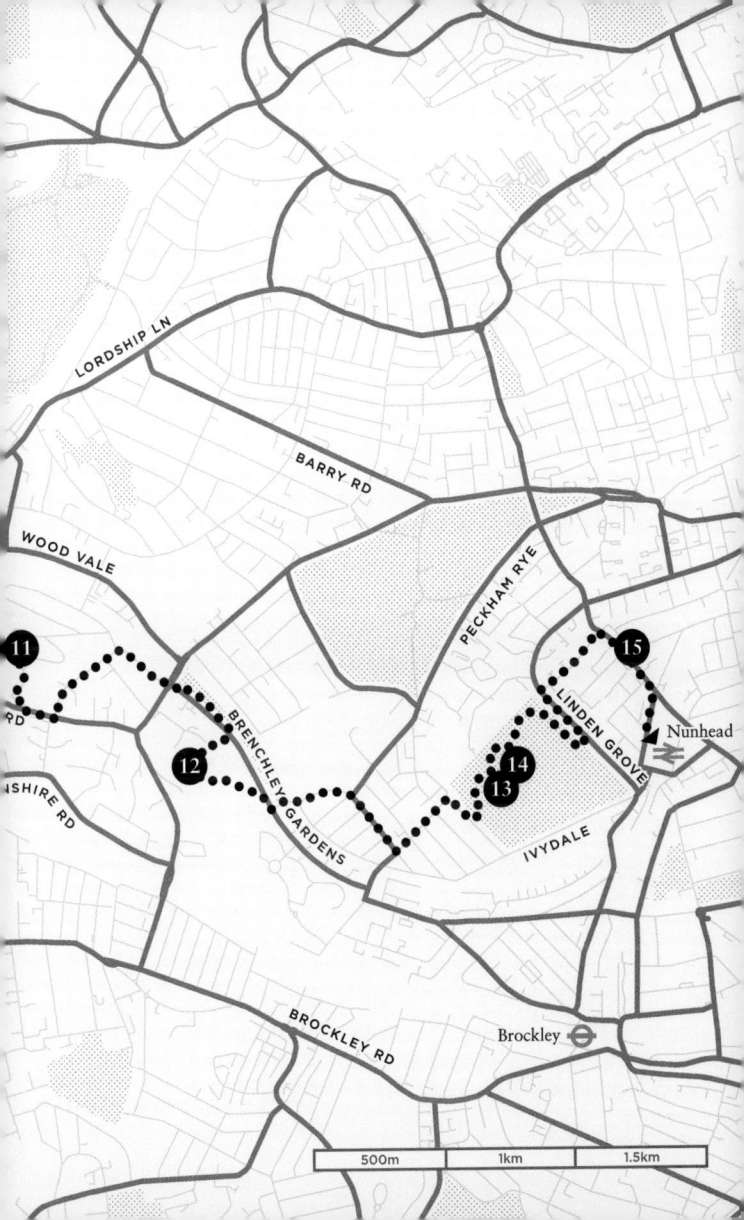

TV tower. The grandiose central steps here ❷ once led to the eponymous palace itself – destroyed by a fire in 1936. Look out for the elegant Italian Terraces ❸ on your left. These pretty stone rows, flanked by three pairs of sphinxes, survived the destruction and are remarkably intact.

After passing the headless statue of Dante ❹ and the steel Crystal Concert Platform ❺ (built in 1997 and nicknamed the 'Rusty Laptop'), exit the park following the Green Chain signs. Turn left, crossing the busy roundabout to Fountain Drive, lined with woodland cul-de-sacs. Passing the immaculate shrubs and stonework of St Stephen's Church ❻, take the gated path opposite Sydenham Hill station and a first left into the cool air of Dulwich and Sydenham Hill Woods – the largest remaining tracts of the Great North Woods that once ran from Deptford to Croydon.

Proceed with the boundary fence on your left until you reach a clearing. Take a hard right, then turn left before the gate to Peckarmans Wood. Traverse ancient hornbeam and oak, turning left at a T-junction with a coppiced fence, now with the metal fence on your right.

Turn right along the old railway track bed towards the eerie boarded Paxton Tunnel ❼. This was once the route of a line between Sydenham and Crystal Palace, and the setting for morbid local legends of old carriages full of skeletons; commuters left to their doom when the route was closed (though other legends

Italian Terraces ❸

suggest this was a different abandoned railway in the park itself).

Take the snaking path over the tunnel to the right – next to the London Wildlife Trust's metal shipping container – and follow the path left at the gate, back through the woods' southern reaches. Head straight, passing a leviathan Cedar of Lebanon and a Victorian folly ❽ of a ruined chapel, descending the rough steps and exiting a gate. To your left is the Cox's Walk Footbridge ❾, from which Impressionist mainstay Camille Pissarro painted a view of Lordship Lane station, reproduced on an information board.

Head right from the gate, bearing right again uphill and exiting on Sydenham Hill road. Turn left and across the roundabout to Eliot Bank. Follow the steep bend down, from which the stately Art Nouveau edifice of the Horniman Museum ❿ looms.

Enter the museum grounds through the colourful Display Garden (with its array of red-hot poker flowers) and the Arts & Crafts-style Sunken Garden, passing the bandstand and the animal pens. There is a sweet market here every Sunday selling street food, coffee, artisan groceries and crafts. Follow a path up the steps, passing the butterfly house and exiting to Horniman Drive. Follow the road past the 'Welcome Aboard' house ⓫ (designed in the image of an ostentatious motor boat).

Keep right as the road snakes downhill, then turn left at the bottom, heading back uphill – extremely steeply – on Canonbie Road; the crest reveals a magnificent view of London's skyline.

Follow the road, crossing at the junction and entering Brenchley Gardens, heady with elderflower come summer. Exit after around 200m and take the footpath onto One Tree Hill **12**. Engage your quads and ascend: on the summit is the Oak of Honour (hence the nearby area's name, Honor Oak). The tree is said to have provided leafy shelter to Queen Elizabeth I when she visited Lewisham in 1602.

Carry on downhill to the main road, turn right and then left onto Kelvington Road. Continue onto Ivydale Road, and snake the streets to the corner of Nunhead Cemetery, turning left down Inverton Road and right down Limesford Road to enter the hallowed boneyard. This is one of London's Magnificent Seven cemeteries, built during the Victorian era to alleviate overcrowding in parish burial grounds when the city's population skyrocketed. Take the left-hand route, turning left at the cod-Grecian tomb of John Allan **13** and past the Romanesque terracotta Stearns Mausoleum **14**. Track through the woods towards the northern exit, keeping the Anglican Chapel behind you.

Hang left and then right down Nunhead Grove, turning east along the green and ending with some deserved carbs at Bar D4100 **15**, south London's best pizza joint. Nunhead station is just a stone's throw further east, up Kimberley Avenue.

10

THE WANDLE TRAIL

A 'lost' river walk through verdant south London

Formerly one of London's 'lost' rivers – historic waterways hidden beneath industrial development and incorporated into sewer systems – the Wandle has been restored and revitalised, with large sections now visible above ground. This truncated version of the full Wandle Trail ambles along the best of it, through some authentically untouristy (but fascinating) green tracts of south London.

Turn left out of the station, then right on North Street. At the Sun pub, cross and enter the Grove through the wall to the right of Mill Lane. Follow the path straight; on your right is Carshalton Ponds ❶, a source of the Wandle. Turn left, past an archaic water wheel and a waterfall, then left again to the park exit.

Turn immediately right, following a track to Papermill Close. Turn right here, cross and continue along the river (a brook at this stage). Turn left on Butter Hill, then right on Mill Lane. Where the road

Length: 11.7km
Walking time without stops: 2 hours 20 mins
Start: ⇌ Carshalton
End: ⇌ Earlsfield

Earlsfield

Haydons Road

QUEENS RD

Colliers
Wood

MORDEN RD

ARTIN WAY

MORDEN RD

CHURCH RD

Mitcham

Carshalton

FRANCISCAN RD

MITCHAM RD

LONDON RD

ROWAN RD

MANOR RD

CROYDON RD

CARSHALTON RD

MIDDLETON RD

EPSOM RD

LOVE LN

ST. HELIER AVE

ROSE HILL

SUTTON COMMON RD

LONDON RD

LE RD

For a digital map, scan
QR code on back flap.

N

1km   2km   3km

becomes River Gardens, feel free to detour through the gate to Wilderness Island ❷: a wild reserve where another branch of the Wandle joins ours.

Otherwise, head straight, tracking the river's bend left and then taking a path on your right off River Gardens to follow its course, signposted 'Wandle Trail'. At Hackbridge Community Garden ❸, exit via a gravel path to Hackbridge Road. Turn right, cross the bridge and turn left again to rejoin the trail, where the scenery becomes more bucolic.

Cross Culvers Avenue – the path onwards is just to the right. As you enter Watercress Park ❹, continue ahead, crossing the Wandle on a wide bridge and taking the first right. Proceed with the river obscured behind bushes and hoardings until you reach Goat Road. Cross, turn right and then left on Watermead Lane, past a silvery Wandle Valley post.

The road soon becomes a track overhung with greenery. After passing astroturfed playing fields, enter a grey metal gate to the Watermeads Nature Reserve ❺, once a medieval water meadow supplying fodder and pasture to cattle. Follow the path left and exit to London Road.

Cross, turn right and rejoin the river path on your left. At the bridge into Ravensbury Park, turn left, following the river's edge past a blue National Cycle Network marker in the shape of an upended fish and a millwheel surrounded by an iron fence. Turn right and then left, passing Ravensbury Park weir soon after.

Morden Hall Park

At Morden Road, turn right and then duck into Morden Hall Park, walking straight along the avenue of beech. Turn left at the T-junction, passing a black poplar behind a coppice fence. Cross a small stream and then a larger arm of the Wandle. Turn right, then right again towards the Wetland Boardwalk **6**: an artificial walkway with raised viewing platforms peering over an ecosystem that is home to herons, snipe, frogs, moorhens, newts and more.

At the boardwalk's end, turn right, crossing the tramline and following the track over a wooden bridge. Continue ahead for almost a kilometre, the track becoming a paved road. On your right, you'll see Merton Abbey Mills **7**.

Built on the site of the mostly demolished medieval Merton Priory, the mills were once a centre of the British textile industry, their factories powered by the Wandle's chalkstream waters. The silk works of department store Liberty were here until 1970. Now, it's a low-key hub of independent craft stores, studios and eateries (family-style Thai spot Ban Yai or zen M.E.D Cafe make good lunch spots).

Cross Station Road and pass through the arch opposite. Turn right and left to rejoin the Wandle Trail. At Merton High Street, a Sainsbury's looms to your right. This was once the location of influential Arts & Crafts pioneer, social activist and writer William Morris's textile and stained-glass factories, Morris & Co **8**.

Above: Wetland Boardwalk ❻
Below: Watermeads Nature Reserve ❺

Turn right on Merton High Street, then left on a path to the right of the Lava Lounge restaurant into Wandle Park ❾. Continue ahead, with the Wandle on your left. Exit the park across a footbridge onto Wandle Bank. Walk right, then ahead through a gap between the house and a brick wall. Follow the unmade footpath, parallel with Bewley Street, past a fake blue plaque ❿ commemorating the spot where hard-nut footballer-turned-actor Vinnie Jones playfully shoved his Wimbledon teammate Dennis Wise into the Wandle in 1989, presumably after one too many shandies.

Cross the water on the footbridge to your right, then turn left, ducking under the low road bridge and continuing across scrubby edgelands. Follow the track diagonally right past a pylon and turn right at the paved path. Turn left through an underpass and follow onwards. The route is now almost entirely straightforward, tracking on for nearly 2km past the apartments, concrete factories, car dealerships and allotments of east Wimbledon, the Wandle drifting on alongside. After a sign describing the clean-up operations taking place on the river, turn right on Trewint Street and then left on Summerley Street. You'll soon hit Garratt Lane – Earlsfield's high street. Parched? Turn left until you reach The Wandle pub ⓫ – an ideal place to neck a pint of local Wandle beer. Merrily quenched, head to the station, back up Garratt Lane.

Morden Hall Park

11

A RICHMOND PARK CIRCULAR

Royal history, rugged charm and over 600 deer

A stomp around the largest Royal Park is a treat in any season, thanks to the abundance of wildlife, botanical splendour and remarkable views. The route there and back – up the hill from rarefied Richmond – is an equally lovely bookend.

Turn left from Richmond station towards the shopping thoroughfare of George Street. Continue following it left at the junctions of King Street and then Water Lane. As the road forks, take the uphill branch of Hill Rise, past a dainty procession of boutiques, florists and galleries.

Ascend past the sculpted Terrace Gardens to your right, with Allan Howe's 1952 fountain sculpture of Aphrodite ❶, dubbed 'Bulbous Betty', their centrepiece. When you reach the top of the hill, opposite Downe House ❷ (former abode of Rolling Stones

Length: 11.5km
Walking time without stops: 2 hours 20 mins
Start: ⊖ Richmond
End: ⊖ Richmond

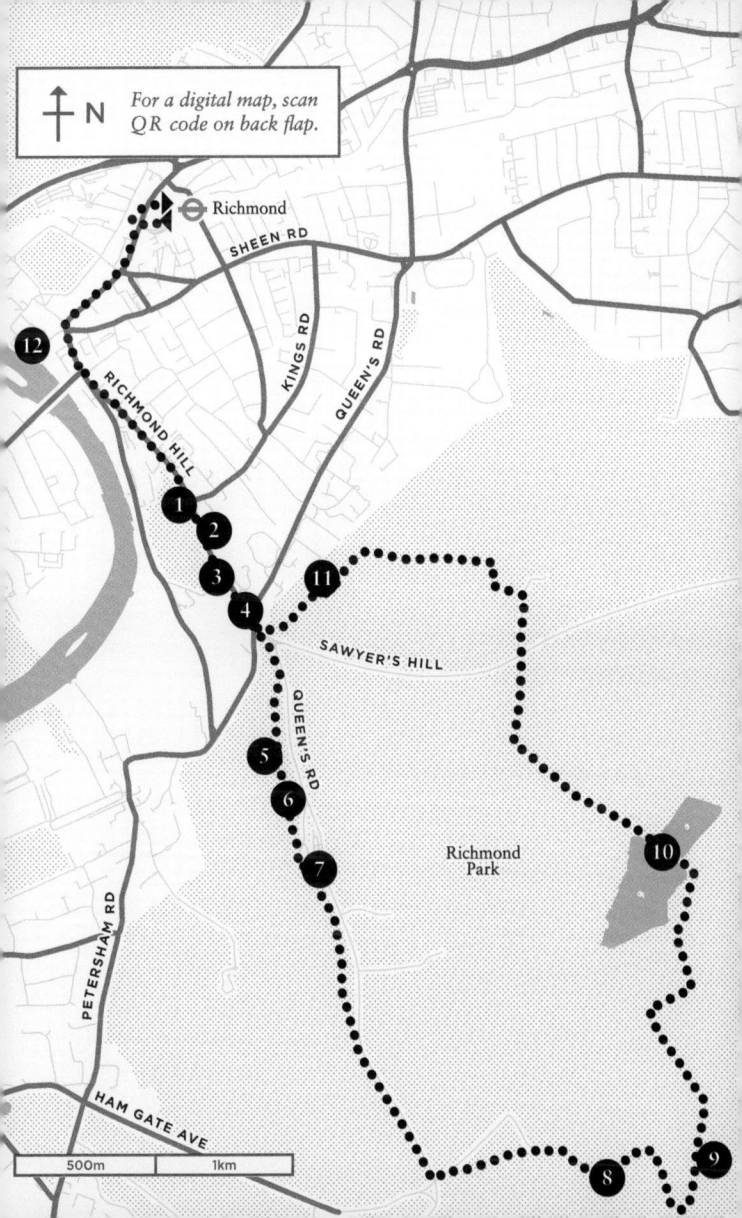

N

For a digital map, scan QR code on back flap.

Richmond

SHEEN RD

KINGS RD

QUEEN'S RD

RICHMOND HILL

(12)

(1)

(2)

(3)

(4)

(11)

SAWYER'S HILL

QUEEN'S RD

(5)

(6)

(7)

Richmond Park

(10)

PETERSHAM RD

HAM GATE AVE

(8)

(9)

500m   1km

singer Mick Jagger), you're met with a wonderful west-facing aspect: painterly Petersham Meadows below, Twickenham in the near distance and the river meandering dreamily between them. Continue past a bronze sculpture of a chimp ❸ on your right until you reach the roundabout with its black iron RSPCA monument ❹ (topped, incongruously, with golden dragons). Cross the road and enter Richmond Park.

The largest of the Royal Parks is a wonder: 2,360 acres of arcadian grassland, undulating hills, shining wetlands, former hunting lodges and wooded tranches. It was developed in 1637 by King Charles I as a deer park; the resident herds are still a truly captivating sight.

After passing the white building on your right (a former hunting lodge, now part of the Royal Ballet School), take the right hand footpath running parallel to the road. Open an iron gate to enter the Poet's Corner Pollinator Garden ❺, its vivid floral displays delighting the seasonal colonies of bees and butterflies. Pass through a covered walkway strung with laburnum and on to King Henry's Mound ❻. This diminutive knoll offers one of London's most quietly spectacular vistas: the gleaming dome of St Paul's Cathedral visible 16km away through a protected gap in the trees (there's an on-site telescope for a closer look).

Proceed along the same path, past rose beds to the lawns outside Pembroke Lodge, turning left to exit through the hedges and arriving at a useful

triple-hit of visitor centre, bathrooms and refreshment kiosk **7**. Turn right, continuing to follow the road from the gravel track's shady vantage. After around a kilometre, turn left across the road, following a wooden sign for the Isabella Plantation. Following the eastward track, immediately take a right-hand fork heading towards a little car park in the trees. A small set of green metal gates next to an information board heralds the entrance to the Isabella Plantation **8**, heady with rhododendrons, magnolias, camellias and a hefty azalea collection. Follow the path to the right of the pond, continuing along the winding gravel path. After 200m, turn left through the shrubs to reveal a second lake, following the path left over a short wooden walkway carved with a grid pattern, greeting crested waterfowl as you go.

Turn left at the north end of the pond, then right at a 'No Public Access' sign. Continuing straight, exiting the plantation at Broomfield Hill.

Turn left, following the iron boundary fence slightly uphill, past Corrett's Copse **9** on your right. Hitting a bisecting track (with another private gate to your left), take the path that closely follows the plantation's eastern edge, then the first, thinner right-hand fork through a sea of ferns.

Cross a sandy track. When you reach the paved road, turn right, then take the second left next to a gargantuan old oak, past a slatted wire fence and onwards to the glistening upper and lower Pen Ponds **10**. Cross

the causeway and continue straight on the sandy track onto open grassland, the sky trailed intermittently by planes descending into Heathrow.

After around 500m, at a red 'No Cycling' sign, turn right and head straight until you reach a paved road. Cross here and turn left when you reach the fence with a sign discouraging the picking of mushrooms. Pass a deer paddock on your left as the track curves to the right; when you reach another broad intersecting path, cross over.

As you head west, the scrub will become bushier on either side, trees rising to block your lateral views. At the next fork, take the gravel track left. Soon, you'll pass Bishop's Pond ⑪ near to the park's northern boundary, the needle-like spire of St Matthias Church rising above rooftops beyond the fence. Continue ahead and Richmond Gate, with an ever-present stream of cyclists and cars, will loom into view.

Retrace your steps back down Richmond Hill to the station. Those in need of a drink should take a short detour down Water Lane at the bottom of the hill. The White Cross ⑫ is a lovely waterside pub with a bizarre USP: its beer garden floods twice each day with the tidal rise of the Thames. Fear not for your sneakers: the pub provides wellies for the uninitiated (and online tide times for the better organised). From here, walk back up George Street towards the station.

12

FOODIES' BERMONDSEY TO BOROUGH

A gastronomic market tour (without the tourist traps)

Timing is everything on this foray from the industrial arches of Bermondsey to thronging Borough Market. Most of the companies and producers around Spa Terminus, a collection of artisan and wholesale traders operating out of the railway arches, throw open their doors to the public on Saturday mornings from 10am-ish until early afternoon. It's a brilliant place to buy artisan groceries and take-home tipples. A couple of hours later, the breweries of the Bermondsey Beer Mile start welcoming day drinkers. The stalls of Maltby Street and Borough Market serve until later in the afternoon. For the full experience, start the walk on a weekend morning.

Turn left out of Bermondsey Tube and left again at St James's Road. Just before the St James of Bermondsey pub is an entrance to Discovery Business

Length: 3.9km
Walking time without stops: 45 mins
Start: ⊖ Bermondsey
End: ⊖ London Bridge

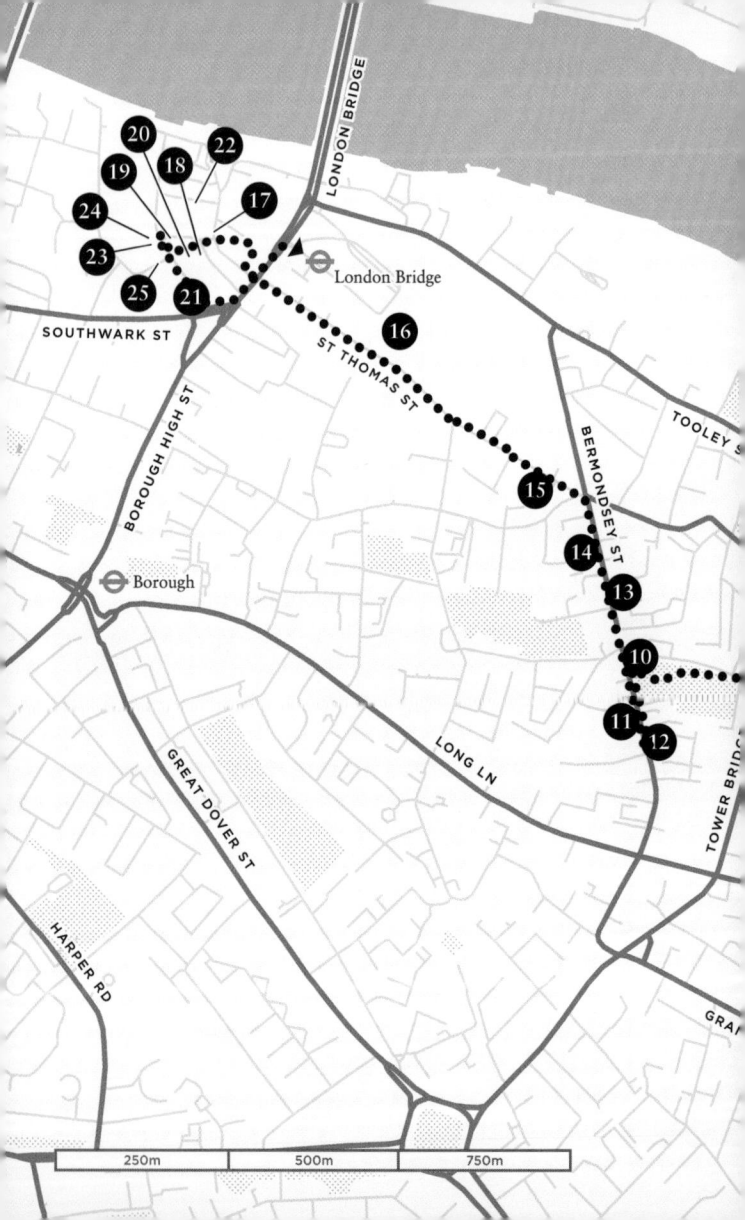

LONDON BRIDGE

London Bridge

SOUTHWARK ST

ST THOMAS ST

BOROUGH HIGH ST

Borough

TOOLEY S

BERMONDSEY ST

LONG LN

GREAT DOVER ST

TOWER BRIDGE

HARPER RD

GRA

20 19 18 22 24 17 23 25 21 16 15 14 13 10 11 12

250m   500m   750m

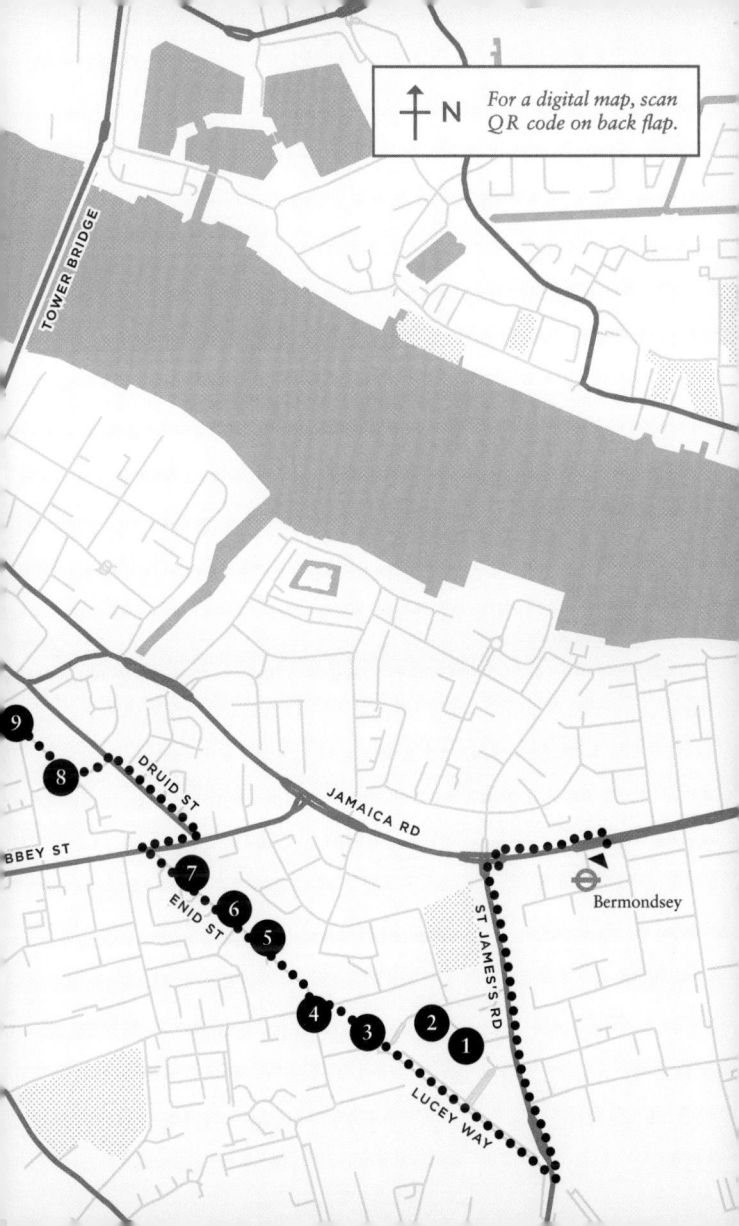

N

TOWER BRIDGE

DRUID ST

JAMAICA RD

BBEY ST

ENID ST

ST JAMES'S RD

Bermondsey

LUCEY WAY

9

8

7

6

5

4

3

2

1

Park, home to Dynamic Vines ❶ – a biodynamic wine importer with a weekend shop selling special bottles to take home and drop-in tastings, for those swinging by a little later. You'll also find Ice Cream Union ❷, one of London's finest purveyors of the chilly stuff.

Leave the yard by the same entrance and continue onwards, passing under the railway bridge, then turn right across the pavement, parallel with the railway lines. A grey gate and sign on your right (opposite the green garages) welcomes you to Spa Terminus ❶. Take your pick of the titbits on offer: Venezuelan arepas at La Pepiá, fine Greek produce at Maltby & Greek, stonking British cheeses at Neal's Yard Dairy, Chinese chilli oils and sauces at Poon's, native breed meats at Farmer Tom Jones, fantastic fruit and veg at Natoora, soil-flecked foraged bits at the Wild Room, non-alcoholic cordials at Gimlet and bread and pastries at the Little Bread Pedlar (among others).

Next, it's time for a crafty tipple: beer, that is. At the end of Lucey Way, turn left on Spa Road. You'll reach the Bermondsey Beer Mile, a strip of railway-arch taprooms that runs from Druid Street to South Bermondsey. On the corner of Rouel Road and Spa Road is the Kernel Brewery's dedicated bar ❹; turn right on Rouel Road and continue onto Enid Street to find some more, including Mash Paddle Brewery ❺, Bianca Road Brew Co ❻ and Cloudwater ❼.

At the next junction, turn right under the railway bridge and left down Druid Street. After passing

the Marquis of Wellington, turn left under the tracks again and enter Maltby Street Market ❽. Once an upstart contender to Borough Market's crown, Maltby Street is now well-established; its assortment of globe-spanning street-food stalls offer a great place to soak up all that beer. Try not to fill up, though – at the end of the Ropewalk is one of this tour's essential stops: 40 Maltby Street ❾. This wine bar is a gem, and the food is as super as the plonk (always order the ever-changing fritters). It's walk-ins only, so you might have to queue, but it's worth the wait.

From here, continue until Tanner Street and turn left, walking on after crossing Tower Bridge Road and entering Tanner Street Park. Cross the park to the northwest exit, eyeballing the oddball totems of the Cornerstone sculpture ❿ on your right (some pouting lips and, er, Peppa Pig among them).

You're now on Bermondsey Street. This buzzy boulevard is a great place to let your lunch settle while you take in a bit of culture, whether big-name modern art shows at White Cube ⓫, wonderful prints, paintings and etchings at the street's two Eames Fine Art galleries (⓬ and ⓮) or natty threads at the Fashion and Textile Museum ⓭.

When you hit the traffic lights on St Thomas Street, turn left and walk past Vinegar Yard ⓯, home to a weekend vintage/makers market, and a fine place to loiter while you rebuild an appetite. Walk on, past the glassy behemoth of the Shard ⓰. At the main road, cross directly over to enter Borough Market: the modern iteration of a trading hub that's existed here for 1,000 years, and a huge part of London's eclectic foodie identity.

The choice is overwhelming. Turn right into the northern section, carving a counter-clockwise route through the stands before heading back across Bedale Street to the western section. Bread Ahead **17**, famed for its doughnuts, is on your right. Other highlights include the Arcimboldo-esque displays at greengrocer Turnips **18**, the Ginger Pig's **19** outrageous sausage rolls and Borough Wines **20**, offering wine on tap. The artery-furring toasties at Kappacasein **21** and the killer Mexican plates at Tacos Padre **22** are also worth dropping by for. Prefer to settle in? The wine-focused, Modern European restaurant Elliot's **23** and the bustling Borough branch of hip Taiwanese micro-chain Bao **24** are marvellous, and stumbling distance from Rimini Gelateria 3Bis **25** for a finisher.

Belly filled, head back down Stoney Street to the main road, entering the subway to London Bridge Tube and station immediately on your left.

13

SOUTH BANK TO THE CITY

A tour of modern and Brutalist builds

London's old-world architectural appeal is undeniable – but the city is also filled with eye-popping contemporary structures. This short walk takes in a few cultural titans before ducking between the gleaming business builds of the Square Mile.

Leave Waterloo by the exit left of the small M&S, crossing the main road onto Sutton Walk. Proceed onto Concert Hall Approach and cross Belvedere Road. Directly ahead of you is the wonderful Brutalist behemoth of Royal Festival Hall ❶. An arts venue built in the mid-1900s, it's the first of the South Bank's grey treasures. Head past the food market and up the steps to the left, turning right as you reach the building's edge. The South Bank Centre and a yellow staircase lie ahead. As you approach, the Hayward Gallery ❷ – another Brutalist gem – will appear to your right.

Length: 5.5km
Walking time without stops: 1 hour
Start: ⊖ Waterloo
End: ⊖ Liverpool Street

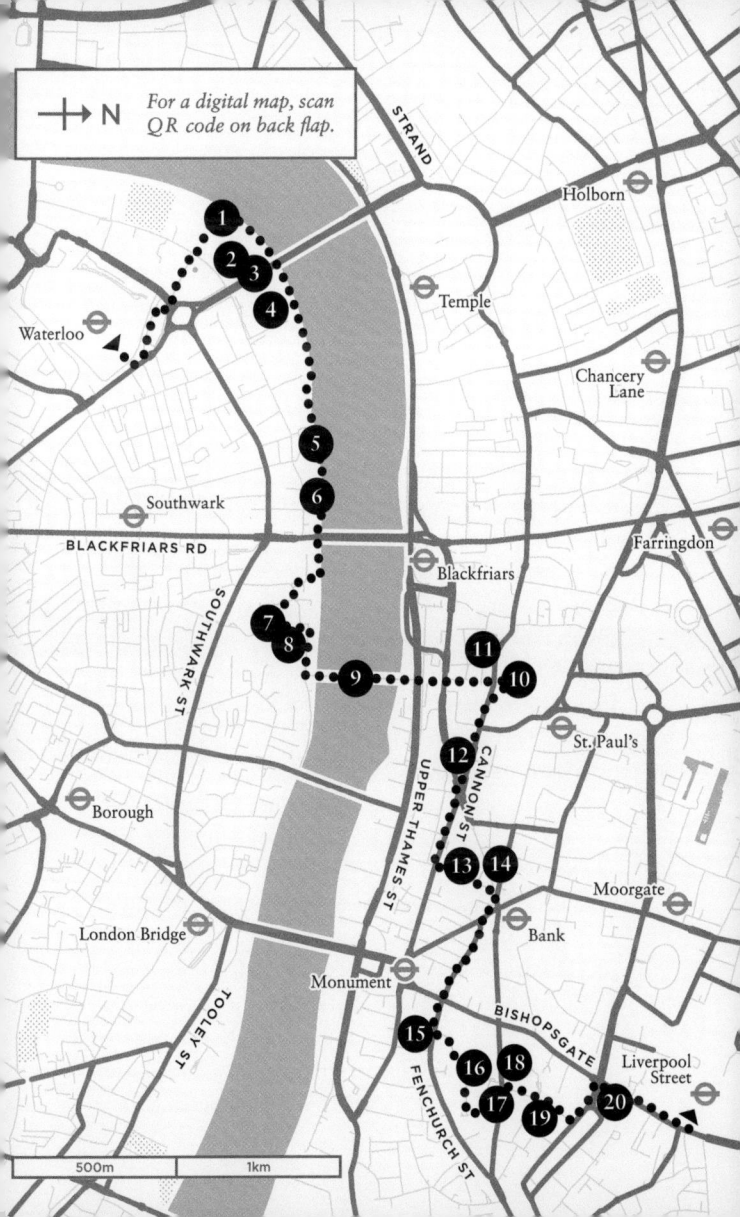

Continue along the riverside of the complex. Descend the stairs from lurid Mexican canteen Wahaca and walk under the bridge, past the BFI ❸. On your right is the National Theatre ❹: another geometric jigsaw of a concrete masterpiece. Designed by Denys Lasdun in the 1970s, the building was despised by modernist mega-fans like architectural historian Nikolaus Pevsner at the time, who declared its grey slabs 'a demonstration against conventional beauty'. Peckish? Both in-house modern British restaurant Lasdun and natty wine and Italianate small plates spot Forza Wine are fantastic.

Press on, passing the Art Deco Oxo Tower ❺, a complex of art and design stores, galleries, apartments and restaurants, and Sea Containers House ❻, a hotel designed by modernist architect Warren Platner in 1974. At street level, you may not realise they're there – but you'll get a better view soon.

Walk under Blackfriars Bridge. Take a right on the Thames Path after the Tube, then left on Hopton Street. Hop across the green to Holland Street to eyeball Rogers Stirk Harbour + Partners' blingy NEO Bankside ❼ apartment towers, with their trademark red vent piping.

Backtrack slightly to pass around the west side of Tate Modern ❽. One of London's most recognisable structures, the former Bankside Power Station was repurposed into the cavernous gallery complex in 2000, and remains a global centre for contemporary

The Royal Festival Hall ➊

The National Theatre **4**
Opposite: Millennium Bridge **9**

art. Cross the tree-dotted concourse and traverse the river via the Millennium Bridge ❾, making sure to glance back down the river as you reach the far side, to take in the Oxo Tower and Sea Containers House.

Here's where everything gets more future-facing. Continue across Peter's Hill and then Sermon Lane. As you reach the road of St Paul's Churchyard ❿, glance left to glimpse the City of London Information Centre ⓫: a jagged slice of silver in stark contrast with the baroque masterpiece of the cathedral itself.

Head right as the road becomes Cannon Street. Cross at the X-shaped junction and take in the curvilinear, retro-futurist edifice of 30 Cannon Street ⓬. Continue ahead, turning left at Walbrook to walk alongside the Bloomberg ⓭ building: designed by architectural godhead Norman Foster, clad in Derbyshire sandstone and covered in bronze 'fins' (parts of which open and close to regulate internal airflow).

Head north. Turn right at Poultry, gazing left to No. 1 Poultry ⓮ – a postmodernist fever dream of rose-pink and yellow stones with a steampunk turret at its centre, housing offices and shops. Turn right, and head slightly right across the large junction onto Lombard Street. Take a left onto Lombard Street proper and cross to Fenchurch Street. The huge pile to your left is 20 Fenchurch Street, otherwise known as the Walkie Talkie ⓯. The undulating, neo-futurist glass exterior once transformed into a giant magnifying glass in the sun, melting a car below

Clockwise from top left: The Oxo Tower **5**;
Tate Modern **8**; *No. 1 Poultry* **14**; *The Walkie Talkie* **15**

(honestly, Google it); it's also home to a lovely sky garden (it's free, but you need to book tickets online).

Turn left at Lime Street, following the street as it curves past the High Tech, dystopian Lloyd's Building **16**, with its lifts, ducts and stairways affixed to the exterior – conceived by Richard Rogers in the late 1970s and genuinely Blade Runner-esque. Continue east along Fenchurch Avenue, glancing left at 52–56 Lime Street **17** – a razor-sharp sliver of a skyscraper nicknamed the Scalpel – then turn left at Billiter Street and left on Leadenhall Street. After taking in the Leadenhall Building **18** – known as the Cheesegrater for its wedge-shaped aesthetic, also designed by Rogers in the High Tech style – turn right on St Mary Axe. At number 30 is the City's arguably best-loved building, the Gherkin **19** – a sinuous neo-futurist plug of a tower, designed by Norman Foster and utterly singular on the London skyline.

Turn left towards Bishopsgate and the final stop, the Heron Tower **20**. Less architecturally nuanced than the previous sights, it nevertheless has a nifty USP in Duck & Waffle: a 40th-floor, 24-hour restaurant that offers panoramic views of the city (particularly at sunrise, sloshing back an early cocktail as you gawp). From here, turn right up Bishopsgate, ducking into Liverpool Street station to head home.

The Gherkin **19** *and the Scalpel* **17**

GREENWICH TO BLACKHEATH

A journey through time (and a tunnel)

This genteel part of southeast London is heaving with historical intrigue, beautiful architecture and expansive green space. This hilly hike explores it all, mostly swerving its hectic, tourist-heavy corners.

Exit the DLR and walk ahead towards the squat, domed entrance to the Greenwich Foot Tunnel ❶. Before descending, amble to the waterfront to take in the view across the river of Wren's baroque Royal Naval College, with the renaissance Queen's House wedged between it and the Observatory on the hill.

Once through the tunnel, pass the Cutty Sark ❷ on your left – a grand, Victorian ship and true Greenwich icon. Proceed on Greenwich Church Street, crossing the junction and turning right down St Alfege Passage, skirting the Hawksmoor church of the same name ❸. This iteration was built on the site of a collapsed

Length: 10 km
Walking time without stops: 2 hours
Start: ⊖ Island Gardens
End: ⊖ Greenwich

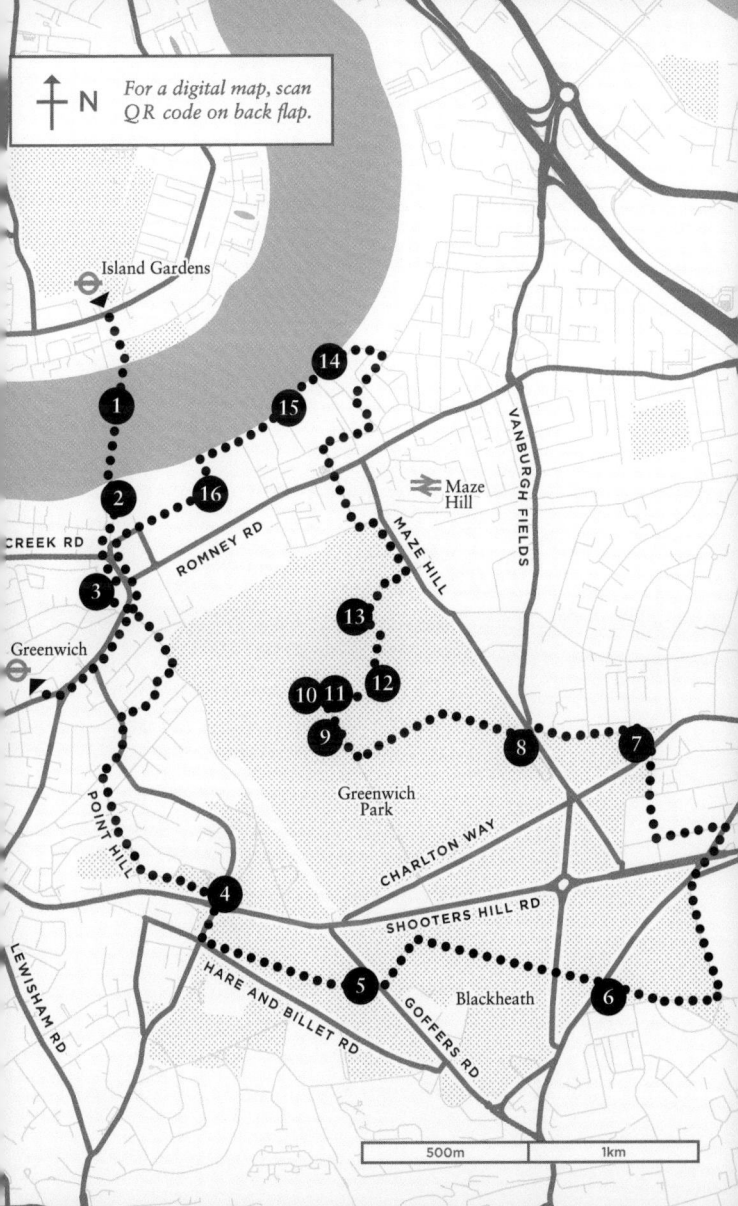

medieval church, under which Alfege himself – a martyred Archbishop of Canterbury – was buried.

Exit to the right of the altar, leaving the church-yard on Greenwich High Road. Turn right and then left onto Stockwell Street, which becomes Crooms Hill. Take the small road right to Gloucester Circus, admiring its handsome Georgian architecture. Leave the Circus at the opposite end of the private gardens, turning left along Royal Hill and left again up the incline of Point Hill. Curve left to West Grove. Leave the road to walk straight across the grass in a south-easterly direction, filling your bottles at the antiquated water fountain and cattle trough ❹ before crossing south onto Wat Tyler Road.

From here, track straight onto the open grass-land of Blackheath, aiming towards the bushy tump of Mounts Pond ❺ to the southeast. The heath has traditionally been a gathering place for protesters, right back to the Peasants' Revolt of 1381 – the largest popular uprising in English history, when 60,000 workers marched on London to protest unfair taxes. The mound by the pond is said to be where rebel lead-ers would give speeches and rally people.

Continue east on the paved path next to the mound, crossing the road onto an unmade trail. Take the next paved route to your right, trudging across the heath's expanse, over Prince Charles Road and Prince of Wales Road to the duck-flecked Prince of Wales Pond ❻. Continue east along the south side of the

Greenwich Foot Tunnel 1

heath. At the corner of the park, turn north along the eastern edge, taking a diagonal right-hand road and crossing the A2 onto Stratheden Road.

Turn left on the gravelled side road of Langton Way, then right on Angerstein Lane. Cross over to Vanbrugh Park and continue on a footpath slightly to your left. In the bushes between here and Charlton Way are 'the Dips' **7**: gravel quarries once used for sourcing ships' ballast. At the main road, turn left and proceed until the intersection with Maze Hill and the boundary of Greenwich Park, passing through an arch in the wall. The cafe ahead, named for the 18th-century writer and composer Ignatius Sancho, serves a tasty strawberry matcha and other brunch classics **8**.

Take the small gate into the Flower Garden, turning diagonally right and passing between neat beds and monstrous pine trees. Exiting the gardens, turn left down a wide paved boulevard, turning right after the car park. On your left is the Royal Observatory **9**, commissioned in 1675 by Charles II and a key location for the study of navigation and the cosmos in the centuries since. It's also the site of the Meridian Line **10**, which has defined time zones worldwide since 1883.

Take the east-leading path into the trees just behind the statue of General James Wolfe **11**. Turn left when you reach the recumbent Elizabeth I oak **12**, then head right on a small track through the undergrowth. Cross a paved path and take the zig-zag route almost directly ahead, up the steps and following railings on

The Cutty Sark ❷

your left to the heady viewpoint of One Tree Hill **13** – an impressive enough aspect that J M W Turner drew a scene from its crest.

Carry on, descending some wide steps and turning right on the paved path at the end. Turn left along the edge of the park, tracing a wall on your right and exiting through a gate next to a hidden garden with an ornately metal-worked gate. Turn left on the road, then right on Greenwich Park Street, crossing the A206. Snake to the river by turning right along Old Woolwich Road, left on Lassell Street, right on Banning Street and left on Pelton Road. Replenish a little energy at the charming Cutty Sark pub **14**, with benches besides the Thames' opaque waters.

From here, follow the river west, past the turreted almshouses of Trinity Hospital **15** (now an OAP's home) and through to the dinky lane of Crane Street. Continue along the water's edge, turning left into the spectacular quad of Greenwich Hospital. Turn right on College Way, passing the Painted Hall **16** (a.k.a., 'Britain's Sistine Chapel', tickets essential) on your left, through the Old Royal Naval College Gardens **17** and exiting at the West Gate. Continue on College Way; when you reach the junction (with Waterstones ahead) turn left and follow the main road as it curves until your end point of Greenwich station and DLR on your right.

Above: Old Royal Naval College **17**
Below: The Painted Hall **16**

15

THAMES PATH TO KEW

A peaceful pad along the river's western course

This long but relaxingly linear walk takes you west along the river, from the grimy inlets and modern waterfront piles of Wandsworth to rarefied Barnes and the wilder riverbanks of southwest London.

Turn right out of the station and proceed under the railway bridge. Cross two sets of traffic lights to enter Smugglers Way (between the bp garage on the left and furniture shop Roche Bobois on the right). Follow the road as it curves left and continue past the waste disposal plant on your right. Enter the pedestrianised walkway and cross the muddy mouth of the River Wandle and then Bell Lane Creek, turning right directly afterwards and following the water until you reach the Thames. Turn left. From here, keeping the river on your right, it's effectively a flat, straight line (though rather more interesting than that sounds).

Pass a raft of homogeneously gleaming blocks on your left, then the Thames Clipper pontoon and

Length: 15km
Walking time without stops: 3 hours
Start: ≋ Wandsworth Town
End: ≋ Kew Bridge

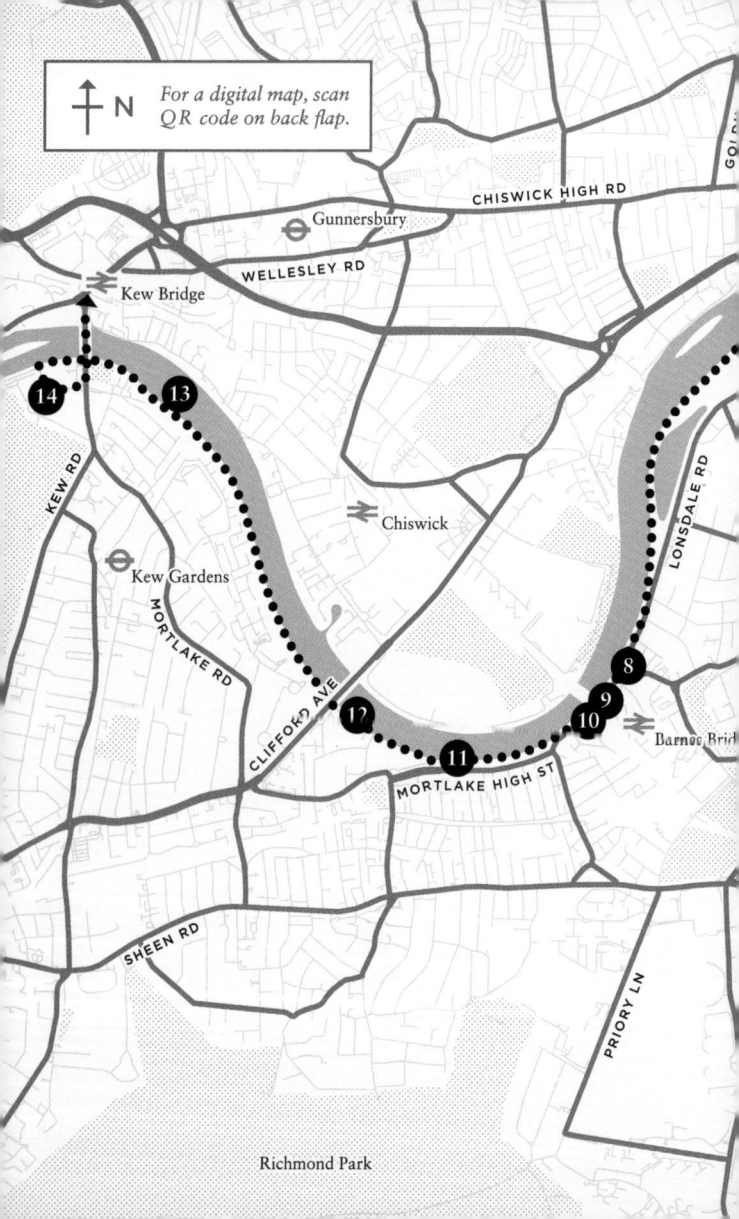

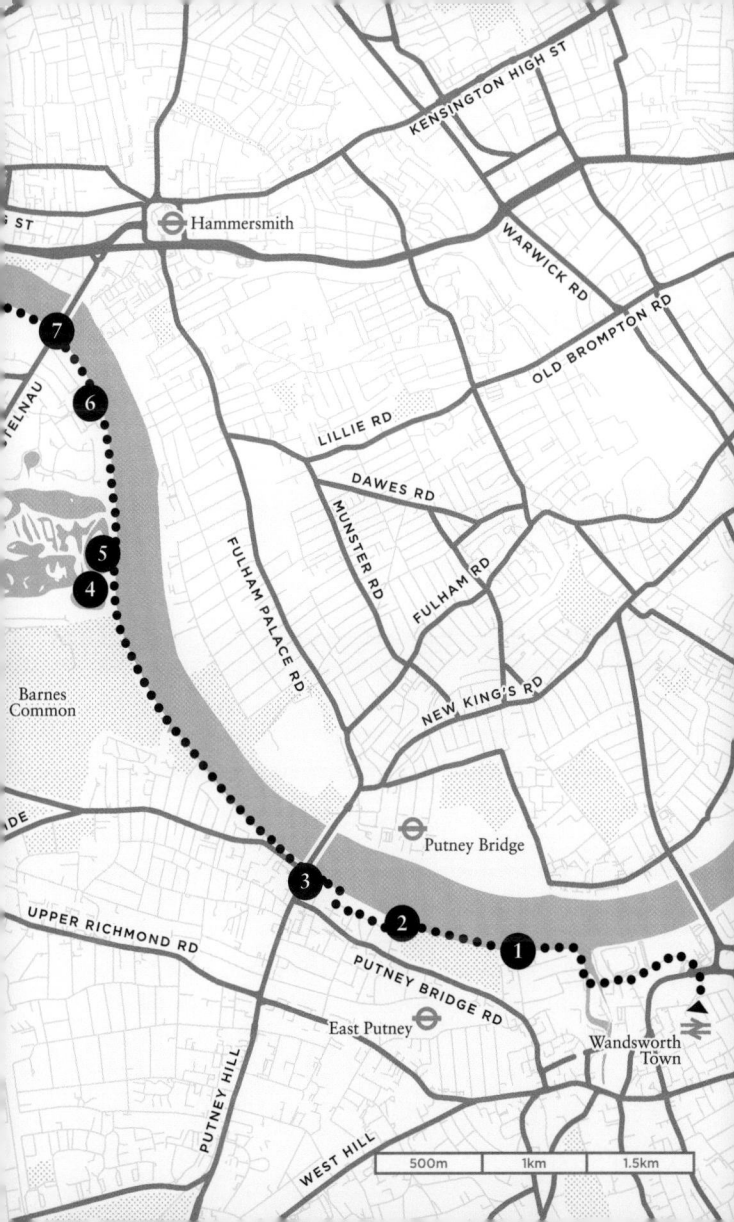

a burnished-green sculpture of two people embracing. Dubbed *The Fall* ❶, this is the first of nine eye-catching pieces by Alan Thornhill along this stretch of waterfront.

Enter Wandsworth Park, turning left at the far end – passing the Scented Garden ❷, a memorial to Fiona Crumley, a local gardener responsible for the winsome beds and planting of the park – and exiting through an arch to Blade Mews. Continue on Deodar Road, following the Thames Path sign right at the T-junction to rejoin the riverside, before swiftly swooping left around St Mary's Church (the adjoining Putney Pantry cafe ❸ is a decent place for a quick caffeine boost). Turn right on the traffic-choked Putney High Street towards the bridge.

Cross left at the second lights, joining the embankment path to the right of Thai Square. The next stretch of riverside is defined by an abundance of public school boating and rowing clubs, their balconied HQs facing onto the water, racing shells stacked in trailers on either side of the track. Continue onto the Putney Towpath, vertiginous black poplar trees swaying above and Fulham FC's Craven Cottage stadium looming opposite. The road soon becomes a wide, gravelled path. At the T-junction, with signs pointing left to the London Wetland Centre ❹ – an enormous collection of wilfully damp natural reserves and habitats – continue straight on. You'll soon pass an obelisk on your left, marking a mile from the start

Harrods Furniture Depository 6

of the Cambridge/Oxford boat race ❺, which takes place each spring, dating back to 1829.

Swiftly on your left is a hulking, terracotta-clad Edwardian pile: the onetime Harrods Furniture Depository ❻. Gently rounding the river bend to the left, mind your head as you duck under the southern end of Hammersmith Bridge ❼ – a resplendent suspension bridge (one of the world's oldest) designed by Joseph Bazalgette and built in 1887. After 2km or so, you'll arrive in Barnes, the foliage-shaded path turning into a paved walkway with iron railings. The Waterman's Arms ❽ – on the corner of the turning to Barnes High Street – is a brilliant lunch stop, easily one of London's nicest gastropubs.

Continue along the riverside, spotting a couple of highbrow blue plaques on your left (to Gustav Holst, 20th century composer of the orchestral suite The Planets at number 10 ❾ and Ninette de Valois, founder of the Royal Ballet at number 14 ❿). Step onto a slatted walkway running underneath the bridge. The well-maintained cobbled path narrows now, running past another plaque – to Elizabethan polymath astrologer and alchemist John Dee ⓫ – as you pass Mortlake.

After a mud-flecked slipway, the path turns back to gravel, becoming paved again at the Ship pub. Proceed along what is now a bona fide road, past a dinky hunk of lichen-covered granite on your right: the 'finishing stone' that marks the end of the

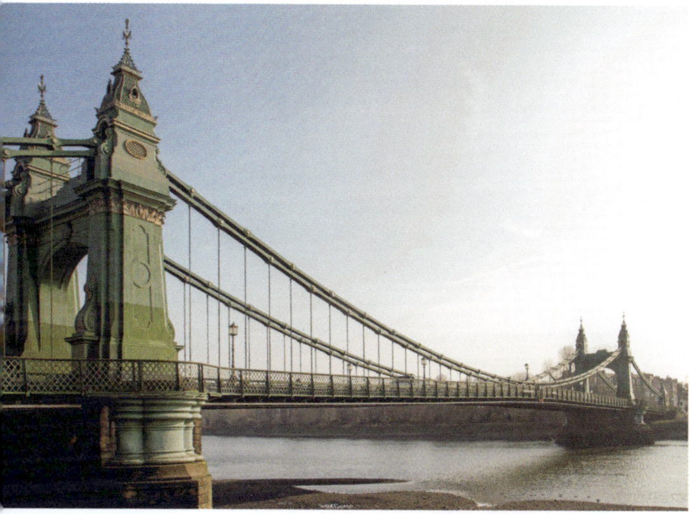

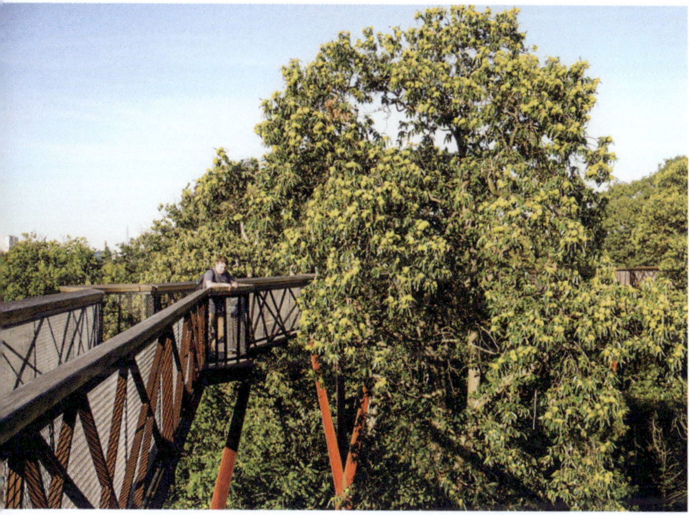

Above: Hammersmith Bridge ❼
Below: Kew Gardens ⓮

Boat Race **12**. Head under Chiswick Bridge and onwards, past pretty, flower-filled cottage gardens on your left and the tree-topped islet of Oliver's Eyot **13** on your right. Eventually you will pass under Kew Bridge and reach the corner of Ferry Lane, with a car park for Kew Gardens **14** just ahead.

If your legs aren't spent, now's a fine opportunity to explore the gardens themselves: 300 acres of botanical wonderment, replete with astonishingly grandiose plant collections, palatial greenhouses, conservatories, lakes, herbariums, libraries, pagodas, temple follies and, best of all, one of Europe's largest compost heaps (the collected lot are a UNESCO World Heritage Site). If that fills your watering can, turn left down Ferry Lane, and then right along Kew Green to the Elizabeth Gate, one of the public entrances to the gardens.

Otherwise, turn left along Kew Green, then left again on the bisecting main road heading back to the river. Cross the water and continue north: Kew Bridge train station can be found to the right of the large road junction.

16

LITTLE VENICE TO CAMDEN LOCK

A dreamy dawdle along the Regent's Canal

This concise, canalside section of the Jubilee Greenway (a 60km-long walking and cycling route devised for Queen Elizabeth II's Diamond Jubilee) has it all: simple navigation, eye-popping architecture, exotic fauna and a fab ice cream to finish it off.

Turn right from the station to proceed along Warwick Avenue. Or, if you simply must have a coffee or snack for the road, first turn left, crossing to Warrington Crescent and ducking onto Formosa Street where the darling Toast cafe ❶ will sort you out, before retracing your steps.

At the junction with Blomfield Road, turn right. As the road curves, pass through a metal gate on your left and turn back along the canal towpath. This triangular body of water is the Little Venice basin ❷ – a junction of three canals, with Browning's Island,

Length: 4.7km
Walking time without stops: 1 hour
Start: ⊖ Warwick Avenue
End: ⊖ Camden Town

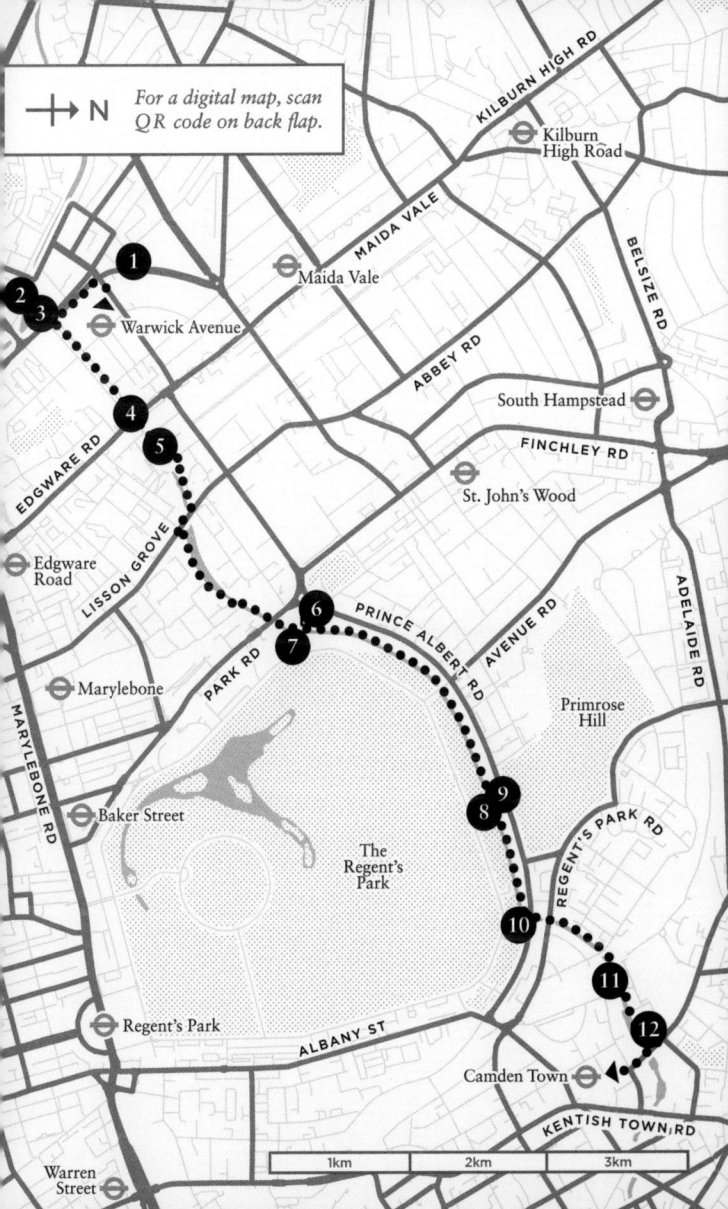

For a digital map, scan QR code on back flap.

N

Kilburn High Road

KILBURN HIGH RD

BELSIZE RD

Maida Vale

MAIDA VALE

Warwick Avenue

ABBEY RD

South Hampstead

FINCHLEY RD

St. John's Wood

EDGWARE RD

Edgware Road

LISSON GROVE

PARK RD

Marylebone

PRINCE ALBERT RD

AVENUE RD

ADELAIDE RD

Primrose Hill

REGENT'S PARK RD

Baker Street

MARYLEBONE RD

The Regent's Park

Regent's Park

ALBANY ST

Camden Town

Warren Street

KENTISH TOWN RD

1km   2km   3km

a dinky outpost for drooping willow and lounging waterfowl, at its centre. Proceed ahead, passing the sweet red-and-yellow awning of the Puppet Theatre Barge ❸: a floating marionette playhouse on a converted 1930s Thames lighter boat. Duck under the blue road bridge, swooning at the vivid houseboats as you go. The path becomes private soon after the bridge: exit onto the road and continue in the same direction on the other side of the iron fence, with the occasional Jubilee Greenway marker embedded in the pavement.

As the road rises, you'll reach the junction with Edgware Road, passing the chic cafe–restaurant Laville ❹, positioned over the canal. A focaccia sandwich at this charming Italian spot makes a perfect lunch. Afterwards, cross to Aberdeen Place, past a blue plaque on the former home of heroic WWII Dam Busters pilot leader Guy Gibson ❺ on your left.

At the end of the road, turn left on Cunningham Place then right through the small estate entrance, and immediately right again to rejoin the canal, walking ahead with it on your right.

At Lisson Grove, with a huge electricity substation ahead, leave the canal to cross the road and turn right. Pass through an arched gate festooned with ducks, fish, cats and boats to walk along the canal once more, this time on its southern bank. Cross again via a green railed footbridge, zigzagging down to the water level and turning left to head under a couple of graffiti-daubed bridges.

Little Venice Basin

Soon after, you'll pass the meticulously land-scaped gardens of Grove House, owned by the Sultan of Oman, on your left ❻. On your right is the monumental Georgian pile of Hanover Lodge ❼, designed by John Nash and once declared by the *Evening Standard* to be 'the most expensive townhouse ever sold in Britain' (yours for a modest £113 million).

This stretch of the Regent's Canal feels particularly restful, dense with a leafy overhanging canopy and waterfowl (not least the colourful Mandarin ducks occasionally seen bobbing along here). It also passes London Zoo – the world's oldest scientific conservation zoo. You can spot some of its characteristic inhabitants from the towpath, including African wild dogs prowling the southern bank ❽ and the bounding primates of Monkey Valley ❾ on the northern one (both just a short walk from Hanover Lodge).

Another 1.5km on, at the Cumberland Basin, is one of the canal's most extraordinary sights: Feng Shang Princess ❿ – a handcrafted floating Chinese restaurant housed in a towering, three-level pagoda, painted bright red and gold, with myriad paper lanterns swaying in the breeze. Follow the towpath left under the road. The surroundings start to feel more urban on the approach to Camden, with stacks of kayaks and other leisure equipment next to the ersatz, unmissable battlements of watersports centre the Pirate Castle ⓫.

After crossing an arched footbridge with claret railings, it's time to pass the threshold to Camden Lock

market on your left. Steel yourself for the crowds. The evergreen tourist tat shops and largely workaday food stalls are an acquired taste (and anathema to a pleasant day out for most actual Londoners), but there are gems to be found. Head straight for Camden Lock Place, directly ahead from where you entered the market, towards Chin Chin Labs ⓬. The sweet bits at this futuristic dessert bar – whose glossy ice cream is created to order with liquid nitrogen – are uniformly excellent, and a perfect way to round off the walk.

Turn right from the shop, and right again onto Camden High Street, heading past the chain restaurants, sartorially dubious t-shirt shops and tightly-packed hellscape of the old Camden Market until you reach Camden Town Tube on your left.

Camden Lock

17

SEVEN THAMES BRIDGES

A west-to-east river slalom with a host of fine crossings

While the Thames Path to Kew (no.15) is green and pleasant, this trek in the opposite direction is more urban, laden with grandiose buildings, historical curios and, yes, seven stately bridges.

Exit Putney Bridge to Station Approach, turning left and left again on Ranelagh Gardens. Walk under the bridge, then turn left on Napier Avenue and right on Hurlingham Road. Enter Hurlingham Park ❶ on your right. Turn left to an oval green, exiting onto playing fields. Walk across them diagonally to your right: you'll see a gate onto Broomhouse Lane halfway along the fence.

Exit and turn right. When Broomhouse Lane becomes Carnwath Road, take the path to the left of the slipway for your first proper view of the river. Follow this back to Carnwath Road and turn right, heading straight – past the mid-century modern Piper Building ❷ on your left, covered in swirling

Length: 12.4km
Walking time without stops: 2 hours 30 mins
Start: ❸ Putney Bridge
End: ❸ Waterloo

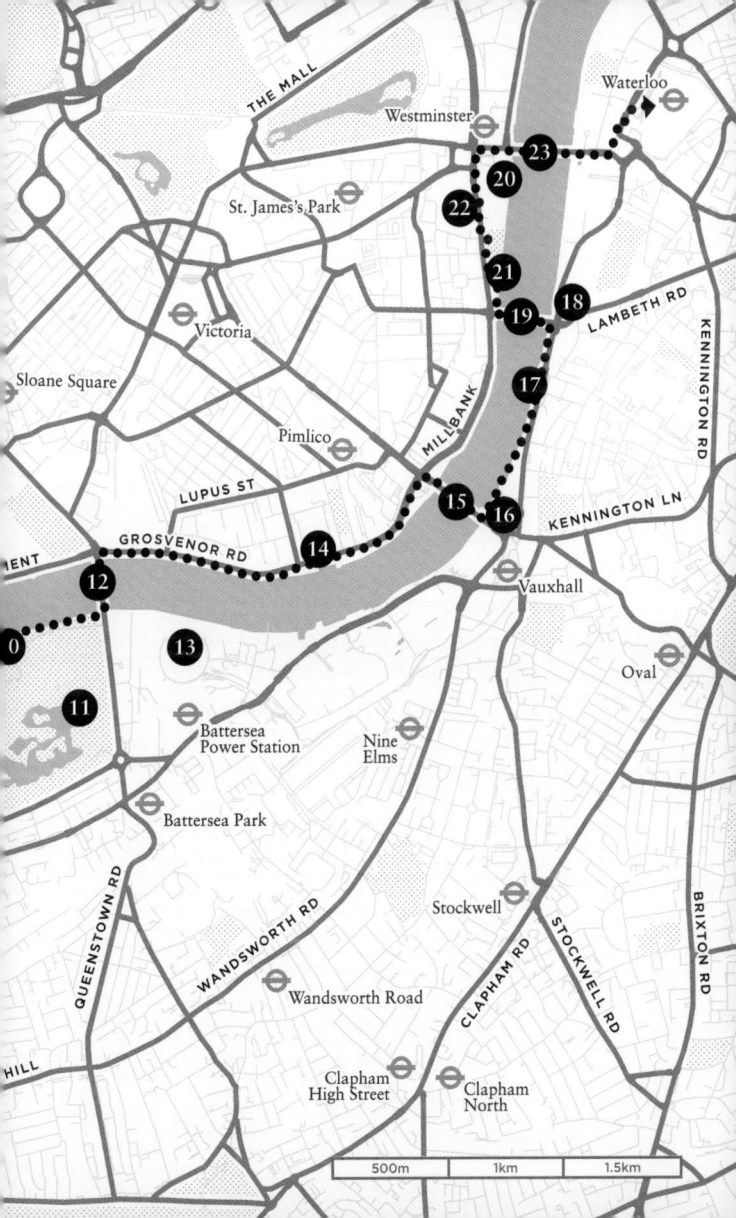

murals at its lower levels – until you reach Wandsworth Bridge ❸, the first of seven.

Cross the bridge. At the south end, take the stairway on your left to reach the river. Turn right and walk past the rocky beach, hulking barges and the brick church of St Mary's, Battersea ❹. After 2.3km – following a clear Thames Path sign – you'll reach the rather grand Battersea Bridge ❺. Cross here and take the steps to your right at its northern edge to rejoin the shore. On this short stretch of the Chelsea Embankment, you'll pass the blocky Chelsea Old Church ❻, an elegant nude statue ❼ by Victorian Royal Academician Francis Derwent Wood and omnipresent amateur artists sketching the Albert Bridge ❽ ahead.

Pass to the right of the statue and climb the steps onto Albert Bridge. Finished in 1873, the bridge had an ominous tendency to shake when crowds walked over it, hence the signs at either end asking troops to break step when marching.

At the south end, turn left into Battersea Park, following the riverbank on Terrace Walk. This zen oasis is dotted with deodar cedar, elm and juniper trees, as well as the London Peace Pagoda ❾ – a stupefying Buddhist temple built in 1984 and featuring gilded bronze scenes of events in the Buddha's life. If you're thirsty for a pick-me-up, cross the lawn south to the parallel drive: the Pier Point Cafe kiosk ❿ does the job, or you could detour further into the park to find the fancier Pear Tree Cafe ⓫.

At Chelsea Bridge ⓬, pass under the road and up the stairs to your right to head across the water. Unbelievably, this stately crossing – demarcated with coats of arms on the pillars at each end – was the site of a vicious battle between rival motorcycle gangs in 1970, who went at each other with chains, knives, sawn-off shotguns and even a spiked flail.

Turn right on the north bank. The stretch to Vauxhall Bridge is traffic-choked, though there are fabulous views of the iconic Battersea Power Station ⓭. The gigantic red-brick building on your left soon after is Dolphin Square ⓮: once the largest block of flats in Europe and home to over 100 MPs at one point in its history.

At the busy intersection, cross the road and turn right on Vauxhall Bridge ⓯. The green-glass-clad postmodern pile ahead of you is the SIS Building ⓰ : the base of the MI6 intelligence service, designed by architect Terry Farrell in thrall to both Battersea Power Station and ancient Mayan temples.

Take the left-hand steps to the waterside just before you reach the SIS, but not before looking down to the river where the bridge reaches land. The 'Effra' sign sits above an old outlet for the 'lost' river that ran from Upper Norwood. The lion's head to its left once held an old mooring ring in its mouth for stricken boats, as well as acting as a kind of early flood warning system; 'When the lions drink, London will sink,' went an old rhyme.

Chelsea Embankment

Head east along the Albert Embankment. Tamesis Dock **17**, a 1930s Dutch barge now converted into a charming bar/pizza spot, is on your left. You could stop here for lunch, or carry on to the Garden Museum **18**, just past the roundabout ahead, home to a superb modern European cafe.

Cross Lambeth Bridge **19**, taking in Big Ben and the Palace of Westminster **20** (a.k.a. the Houses of Parliament) just further up the river – seat of British democracy, UNESCO World Heritage Site and Gothic Revival icon. After the bridge, cross into Victoria Tower Gardens South, past the Buxton Memorial **21** which commemorates the 1833 emancipation of enslaved people across the British colonies. Leave the gardens onto Millbank at their northeast corner, turning right and eyeballing the hallowed heights of Westminster Abbey **22** on your left, before dodging tourists and cheering/lambasting whichever protesters have taken up on Parliament Square that day.

Turn right after Parliament to cross Westminster Bridge **23**, with its honking bagpipers and tuk tuk hordes. After passing St Thomas's Hospital, turn left on York Road and head straight. Waterloo station and Tube will be on your right.

18

A ROYAL PARKS RAMBLE

Pelicans and palaces in central London

This amble through four of London's Royal Parks offers a mix of evocative public artworks, stately cachet and sculpted flower gardens. It also manages to almost entirely avoid any roads: a rare novelty in central London.

Exit St James's Park station and head north to Queen Anne's Gate, continuing on the pedestrianised walkway ahead. Cross Birdcage Walk and enter St James's Park. Continue past the information board and ornate drinking fountain. You'll soon reach the Blue Bridge **1**, heaving with tourists taking in the lake's languid waters, with Buckingham Palace to the west. Instead of crossing, turn right, following the water's edge. As you near Horse Guards Road, the lake opens up. It is dreamlike: pastel-coloured pelicans and Canada geese drifting on the water, herons resting on the rocks and the delightful 18th-century Duck Island Cottage **2** (once home to the park's duck keeper) in the background.

Length: 7.8km
Walking time without stops: 1 hour 30 mins
Start: ⊖ St James's Park
End: ⊖ Lancaster Gate

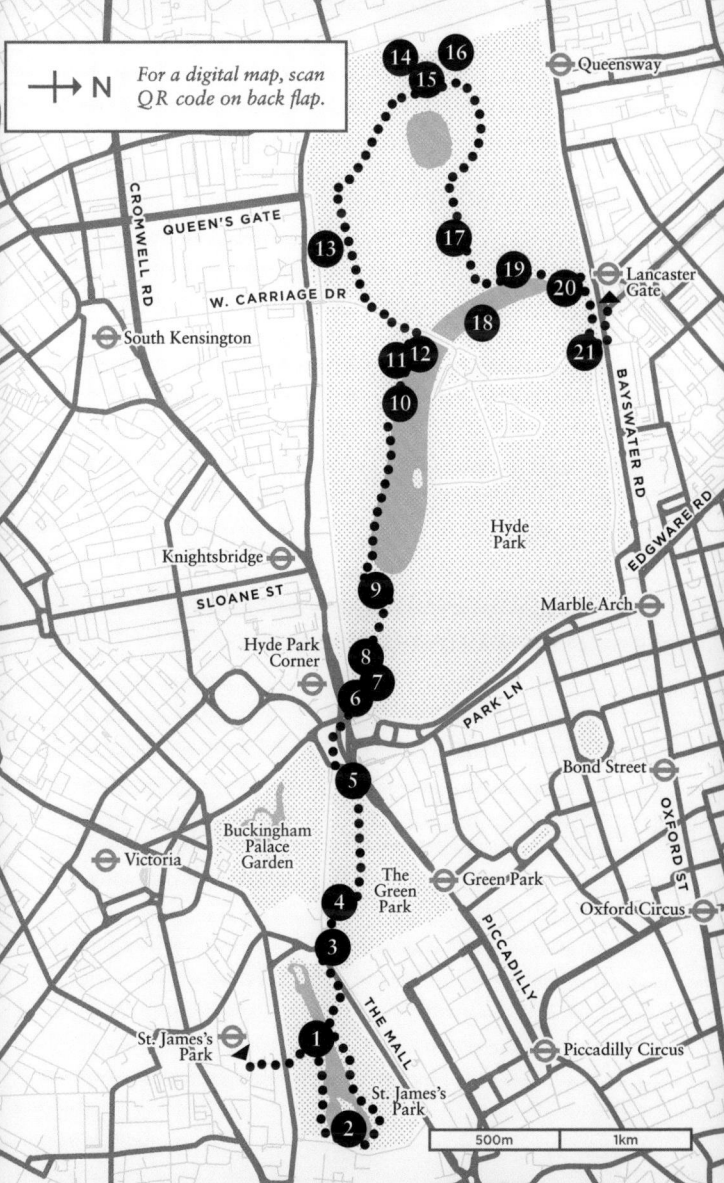

N

QUEENSWAY

CROMWELL RD

QUEEN'S GATE

W. CARRIAGE DR

South Kensington

Lancaster Gate

BAYSWATER RD

EDGWARE RD

Hyde Park

Knightsbridge

SLOANE ST

Marble Arch

Hyde Park Corner

PARK LN

Bond Street

OXFORD ST

Buckingham Palace Garden

Victoria

The Green Park

Green Park

Oxford Circus

PICCADILLY

St. James's Park

THE MALL

Piccadilly Circus

St. James's Park

500m   1km

Follow the water past the cottage's chocolate-box gardens. Head west, past the cafe and back to the water.

Turn left as the waterside path rejoins an inland one, then take the second right to the Mall, past one of the Regency-style 'floriferous shrubberies' (flowering shrub gardens). Turn left on the grand thoroughfare, lined with billowing Union Jacks. Before you reach Buckingham Palace, hang right through the meticulous Constitution Hill Memorial Garden ❸ (planted in honour of Queen Victoria in 1901, after her death).

After the wrought iron Canada Gate, turn right into the Green Park. Head northwest, taking in the minimalist slabs of the Canada Memorial ❹, commemorating members of the Canadian forces who lost their lives in WWII, on your left. Continue on and turn left. When the path ahead forks into three, continue along the middle path, heading west across the park, past wilfully unkempt wildflower meadows.

After the Bomber Command Memorial ❺ – dedicated to RAF pilots from the Second World War – turn left, and then right across the traffic lights to Apsley Way. Pass under Wellington Arch, hanging right and crossing two more sets of lights to enter Hyde Park.

Cross South Carriage Drive and turn left along the sandy track of Rotten Row, taking the first diagonal right to enter the fragrant, technicolour Rose Garden ❻. Pass the robust Boy and Dolphin fountain ❼, continuing west past the daintier fountain sculpture of

St James's Park

St James's Park

Diana, Roman goddess of the hunt **8** and a series of metal arches on your left. Exit the garden, continuing along the same path until you reach a T-junction, turning hard left and passing the dreamy lawns and levels of the Serpentine Stephen Waterfall **9**.

Turn right at the main track and head uphill to meet the lower shore of the Serpentine itself. Turn left and follow the gently lapping water, past the Lido **10** (open in the summer months and well worth a dip) and its neighbouring cafe, replete with a dainty clocktower.

Keep walking until you reach the Diana, Princess of Wales Memorial Fountain **11** – an abstracted, oval stream cast in granite – and sculptor Simon Gudgeon's 2009 Serenity **12**, a giant waterbird rendered in patinated green bronze. Head up to the road and turn left, passing the Serpentine Gallery, taking the next right into Kensington Palace Gardens. Proceed slightly left along a path signposted Flower Walk, entering the vibrant fenced area (originally designed for King George II's queen, Caroline, in the early 1800s) just as the magnificent spires of the Albert Memorial **13** rise directly to your left.

Reaching an open paved area lined with benches, turn right through the gate. Follow the sign towards Kensington Palace, heading up a wide path until you reach the busy Broad Walk. Turn right, past Kensington Palace **14** on your left. To its right-hand side is the Sunken Garden **15**, with a bronze memorial statue of Diana, Princess of Wales – lambasted for 'aesthetic

The Wellington Arch, between the Green Park and Hyde Park

awfulness' by the *Guardian* art critic Jonathan Jones in 2021. Judge for yourself.

Opposite the baroque Orangery restaurant **16** – an apt lunch stop – take a path to your right, following the gentle clockwise contour of the Round Pond. Take a 90-degree turn left when you've circumvented half of the pond, heading west, past Physical Energy, a horse and rider sculpture created by George Frederic Watts, erected in 1907 **17**. Take the nearest onward path until you reach the recreational lake of the Long Water; Henry Moore's tooth-inspired *The Arch* 1979–1980 sculpture **18** is visible on the opposite bank.

Turn left, past the statue of JM Barrie's Peter Pan **19** (a palpably melancholy sight for anyone who's seen *Hook*). You'll soon reach the pools and fountains of the Italian Gardens **20**. The point at which they meet the Long Water's glistening levels, dotted with swans and green algae, is arguably the park's most painterly scene.

Continue straight, turning right at the cafe and passing Buckhill Lodge. At North Carriage Drive, peer through the gate to the right of the entrance to Victoria Lodge: the tiny headstones, heartbreakingly inscribed, are those of a Victorian pet cemetery **21**. Exit onto Bayswater Road and turn left: Lancaster Gate Tube is on the opposite side of the road.

19

HAMPSTEAD AND THE HEATH

Majestic urban wilderness

Arguably London's greatest natural expanse – and certainly one of its most decorous neighbourhoods – the Heath and its surrounds offer it all: wild greenery, perfect ponds, lost rivers, stonking views, famous denizens and some of the city's most fêted modernist architecture. Don't forget your swimmers.

From Hampstead station, head uphill to Heath Street and Whitestone Pond ❶. This is one source of the River Fleet, which runs to Blackfriars (now largely underground). Turn right at the roundabout and follow a sign for the Vale of Health. Walk along the dirt path, turn right at the end and cross the gorse-lined clearing towards a gap in the trees. This is the Vale itself, a micro-village cosseted within the Heath's shrubbery, former residents of which include DH Lawrence and Bengali painter-poet Rabindranath Tagore.

Length: 7.5km
Walking time without stops: 1 hour 30 mins
Start: ⊖ Hampstead
End: ⊖ Belsize Park

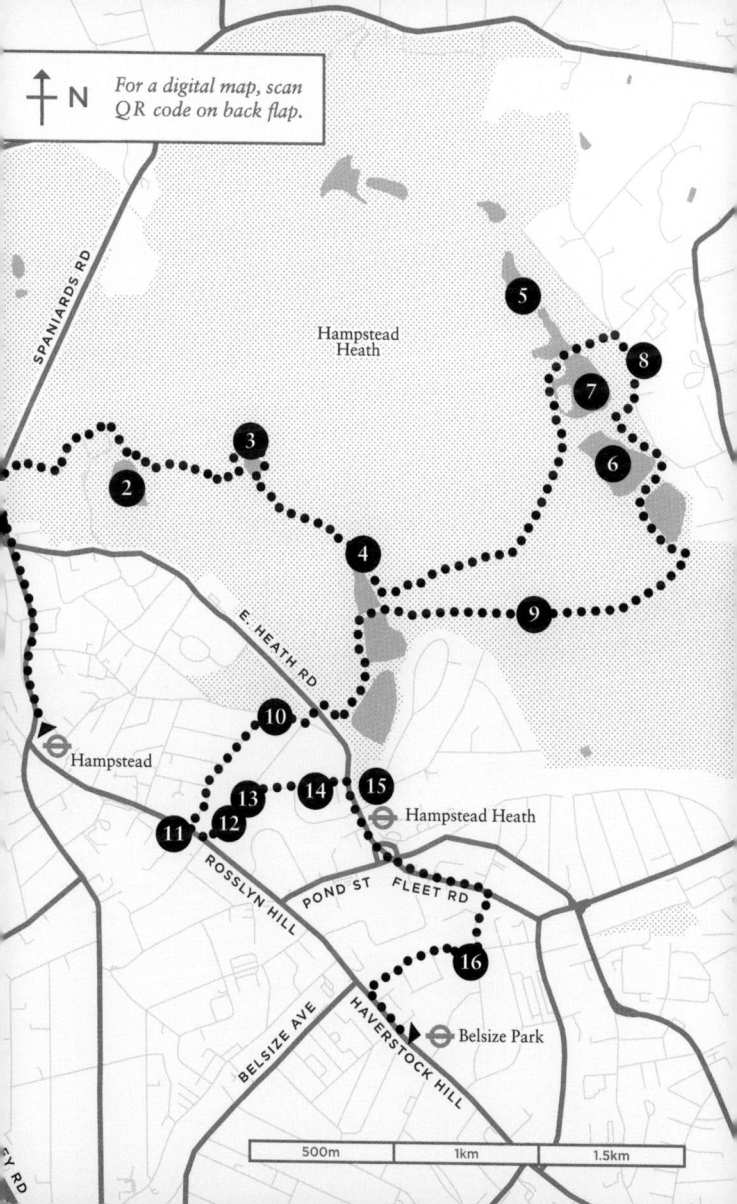

N

For a digital map, scan QR code on back flap.

Hampstead Heath

SPANIARDS RD

E. HEATH RD

ROSSLYN HILL

POND ST

FLEET RD

BELSIZE AVE

HAVERSTOCK HILL

FY RD

Hampstead

Hampstead Heath

Belsize Park

2

3

4

5

6

7

8

9

10

11

12

13

14

15

16

500m   1km   1.5km

Turn left, past Lavender Cottage, the brick terrace of the Gables and a caravan park owned by the Abbott family (Irish showmen resident here for over 150 years). Follow the park's fence around to the right, noting the iron City of London Council bollards – demarcating, until 1965, the official 'edge' of London. You are now at the border of the Heath – about 100m down this path is the shining Vale of Health pond ❷. When you reach it, take the path into the woods on your left and veer immediately right. The unconstrained wildness here is a vision, a canopy of chestnut trees dappling sunlight onto the forest floor (pleasant weather depending).

Tread past a gnarled oak into a clearing, tracking downhill into denser woodland until you reach a small right-hand bridge over a muddy brook – this is the Fleet. Don't cross yet; turn left past another oak, traversing a tiny bridge and continuing to a boggy expanse, kept on one's right. Turn left up a steep incline, from which you'll see the Viaduct Pond ❸, one of the Heath's lesser-known bodies of water. Keeping the rails on your right, head uphill and cross the viaduct, taking in the pretty southern section of the pool (and the wilder northern one). Follow the water's edge until you reach the far side, with its spectacular vantage of the bridge in its full Victorian glory.

Head left, across an avenue of trees, to a grassy meadow. Turn left down the bowl of the hill into the woods. On the right, the murmur of lively bonhomie

and splashing announces the Mixed Bathing Pond **4**. This is one of the three wild swimming spots on the Heath, and worth a dip (prebooking essential at peak times). Follow its border uphill along a footpath and east across the Heath for almost a kilometre. There is a row of ponds on the far eastern side, among them the Kenwood Ladies' **5** and Highgate Men's **6** Bathing Ponds (again, prebooking recommended), and the Model Boating Pond **7** (swimming is prohibited here, but the bank makes an ideal picnic spot).

Directly east of the Model Boating Pond, at 44 Millfield Lane **8**, is a complex of heavily CCTV-monitored buildings. Technically part of the Russian Federation owing to its use as the Russian Defence Office, these were long thought to be a base for Russian spies. Indeed, 20th-century novelist John le Carré, who lived in Hampstead, used the Heath as a setting in several of his Cold War-era espionage novels.

Head back the way you came via the lofty viewpoint of Parliament Hill **9**, the city spreading out like a toytown below. Aim west, turning left after the Mixed Pond dam and past pond numbers 2 and 1.

London's creative milieu has flocked to the Heath for generations, and there are several famous residences on the surrounding streets. Turn left towards the car park and cross the intersection of East Heath and South Hill Roads. Just outside the Heath, you'll find 2 Willow Road **10**: a modernist marvel designed in the 1930s by architect Ernö Goldfinger.

The Mixed Bathing Pond 4

Continue along Pilgrim's Lane. At Rosslyn Hill, U-turn past Ottolenghi **11** – an ideal, cosmopolitan lunch stop – and onto Downshire Hill, past a plaque to Muppets puppeteer Jim Henson **12** and the futuristic Hopkins House **13**, home of two High Tech architects. Sweep right onto Keats Grove and past the former home of the Romantic poet **14**, reaching South End Road and a strip of shops.

The Magdala **15** on South Hill Park is a grand place for a pint. The tiled wall outside is dinked with a bullet hole created by Ruth Ellis in 1965, when she shot her lover and subsequently became the last woman in Britain to be executed by the crown. The hole is visible around shoulder height, beneath the third window from the left of the main door.

Head south from Hampstead Heath station to Fleet Road (named for the aforementioned river). Turn right onto Lawn Road, towards the gleaming Isokon Flats **16** – a hub of experimental pre-WWII apartments once home to Bauhaus bigwigs Walter Gropius and László Moholy-Nagy, plus Agatha Christie. There's an informative, resident-run museum on site. Backtracking slightly, find the path through Belsize Woods – head through, along Aspern Grove and left on Haverstock Hill, ending your stroll at Belsize Park Tube.

Isokon Flats **16**

20

THE PARKLAND WALK

Secluded former railway line through north London

Following part of the disused railway line between Enfield and Finsbury Park, the Parkland Walk is a fertile and easily traversed route through these pretty tracts of north London – with a few surprising distractions along the way. We've added a pleasant prefix at Alexandra Palace, before the path starts properly at Muswell Hill.

Exit the station and turn left, cross the narrow footbridge and walk to Bedford Road, past a dainty community garden behind railings. Turn left again at the road, entering the sprawling green of Alexandra Palace Park. Follow the road past the park's entrance sign and take the second left turn, continuing past a sandy petanque area.

Stay on this path, enjoying the contrast between the park's meadow-like folds and the rooftops of residential north London. Peek through the trees to your right and you'll spot the elegant rose window of the

Length: 8km
Walking time without stops: 1 hour 30 mins
Starts: 🚋 *Alexandra Palace*
Ends: 🚇 *Finsbury Park*

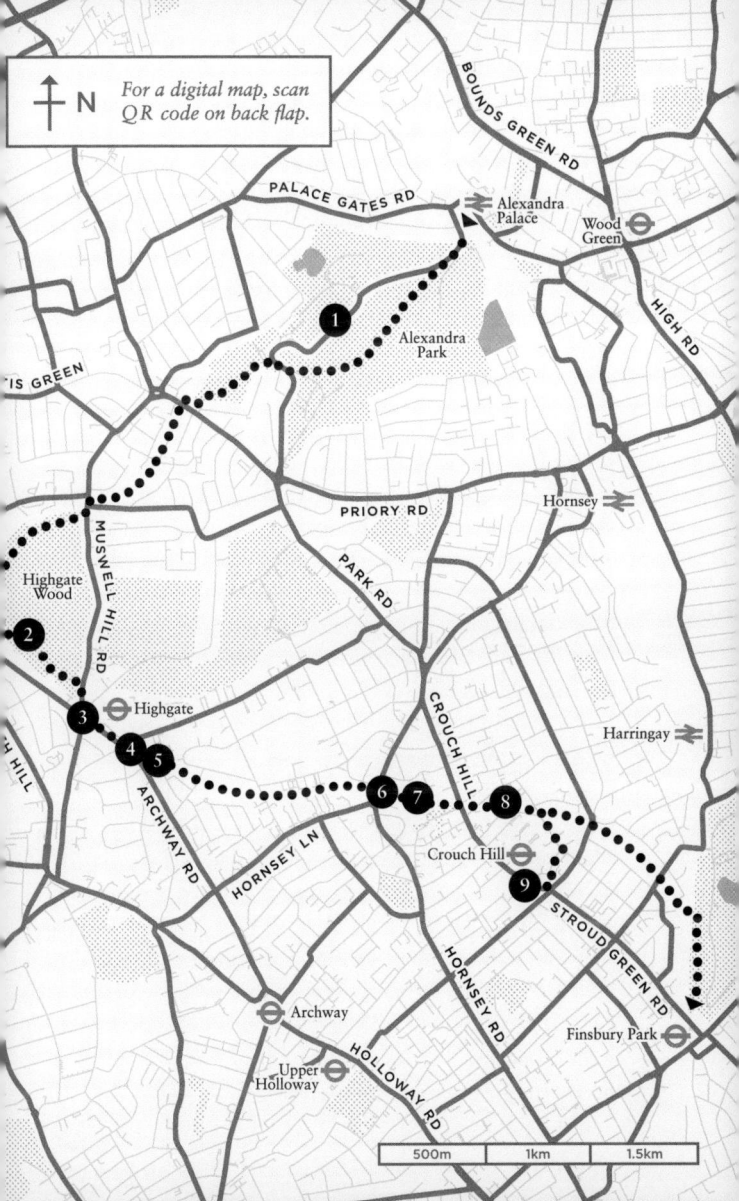

For a digital map, scan QR code on back flap.

BOUNDS GREEN RD

PALACE GATES RD

Alexandra Palace

Wood Green

HIGH RD

1

Alexandra Park

IS GREEN

PRIORY RD

Hornsey

MUSWELL HILL RD

PARK RD

Highgate Wood

2

CROUCH HILL

Harringay

3

Highgate

4 5

ARCHWAY RD

HORNSEY LN

6 7

8

Crouch Hill

9

STROUD GREEN RD

H HILL

Archway

HORNSEY RD

HOLLOWAY RD

Upper Holloway

Finsbury Park

500m   1km   1.5km

Palace itself **❶** – conceived by architect Owen Jones in 1859 as a 'Palace for the People', opened in 1873 and subsequently used both as entertainment venue and BBC transmitting station.

Continue in this direction, re-entering the woodland, until you reach a road: Alexandra Palace Way. Turn right uphill and cross the road, following the sign to Muswell Hill by the bus stop. Proceed to a clearing and take the left-hand path through a shady avenue of linden trees. Follow the paved path left between iron railings and a yellow-roofed overpass, continuing on a gravel track lined with knee-high woven branch fences. The path quickly opens to the sky again, with slanted, rusted railings pointing to the panoramic expanse of central London to the southeast on one side, and the hum of suburbia to the other.

After the canopy closes in once again, you'll soon find a series of steps on your left leading to Cranley Gardens, once home to serial killer Dennis Nilson. Turn left when you reach the road, entering Highgate Woods on your right. The official Parkland Walk route, which starts here, runs parallel to the path you're on, outside of the woods' boundary fence. You'll rejoin it later.

The path through this peaceful ancient woodland is straightforward, offering striking sylvan charm compared to the relative hubbub of Ally Pally (as it's fondly known). Passing veteran oak, hornbeam and beech trees, listen out for the thwack of leather on

Highgate Wood

willow: a cricket pitch **2**. Keep it to your left and trudge on, noting the bat boxes perched high in the boughs. Continue past the playground and loos and then exit at Gypsy Gate.

Head uphill, turning left at the Woodman pub (great for a snifter) **3**, continuing past the sunken Highgate Station, mid-century antiques emporium Gonnermann and the winsomely shabby Boogaloo **4** pub (replete with its own radio station). Turn left down Holmesdale Road and take the next left to rejoin the Parkland Walk – this tranche of the route follows part of the long-departed railway line between Edgware and Finsbury Park, constructed in the 1860s and abandoned just over a century later.

This wholly linear part of the walk is 2.7km in length. A notable prefix is the delightful Wildlife Trail **5**: a fenced area immediately on your left with a fecund and biodiverse array of micro-landscapes, from a woodpile to a dinky pond.

The walk itself is hugely tranquil, perfect for a lazy Sunday afternoon stroll. Around halfway, where the track intersects with Crouch End Hill road overhead, you'll see the old platforms from the otherwise vanished Crouch End station, engulfed in dense foliage **6**. A little further on, in the brickwork, look out for the Spriggan **7**: an unearthly sculpture of a sprite, inspired by a figure in Cornish folklore and installed as a paean to Crouch End's history of permaculture in 1993.

Alexandra Palace 1

After ducking under Crouch Hill road, you'll reach a steep, bare swathe of hillside lawn to your left known as the 'acid grassland' ❽. Though innocuous, this area is laden with diminutive biodiversity, from an abundance of fascinating flora – such as sheep's sorrel, with its tiny red flowers and arrowhead-shaped leaves – and fauna, like Formica cunicularia, a pan-European species of ant first recorded here in 1914 (and happily proliferating ever since).

It's worth a detour at the next road intersection to reach the walk's best lunch stop. Head onto Mount Pleasant Villas towards Crouch Hill to Max's Sandwich Shop ❾: the city's finest purveyor of creative, doorstep-size carb-bombs, stuffed with cheffy takes on the trad chicken caesar, or ham, egg and chips (and so on). Retrace your steps to rejoin the route.

The walk continues past an abandoned signal post, brambles, banks of goat willow and violet buddleia bushes, before crossing a graffiti-laden footbridge into Finsbury Park itself. Turn right, past the tennis courts and skate ramps, ending at Finsbury Park station and your ride home.

IMAGE CREDITS

Page 2: Getty Images; page 4 © CAMimage / Alamy; page 5 © Pedro Ramos; page 6 © Lee Martin / Alamy; page 7 © David Jacobs. Square Mile: Image 1 © Marco Kesseler; Image 2 © Dr Johnson's House; Image 3 © David Iliff; Image 4 © Taran Wilkhu; Image 5 © Nikreates / Alamy. Clerkenwell and Beyond: Image 1 © Ian Crowson / Alamy; Image 2 © Simon Turner / Alamy; Image 3 © Eric Nathan / Alamy; Image 4 © Stefan Johnson; Image 5 © Taran Wilkhu. Bohemian Soho: Image 1 © Jon Ingall / Alamy; Image 2 © RayArt Graphics / Alamy; Image 3 © David Richards / Alamy. Literary Bloomsbury: Image 1 © Barbara West / Alamy; Image 2 © Vera_Janev; Image 3 © Siobhan Doran-VIEW / Alamy. East London through the Ages: Image 1 © Guy Montagu-Pollock; Image 2 © B.O'Kane / Alamy; Image 3 © Homer Sykes / Alamy; Image 4 © Charlotte Schreiber; Image 5 © Rachael Smith Photography Ltd; Image 6 © Chanel Irvine. The Line Art Trail: Image 1 © ZipWorld; Image 2 © Will Corder; Image 3 © vassilis skopelitis; Image 4 © Ada Ihebom. The Lea River: Image 1 © Julio Etchart / Alamy; Image 2 © Marco Kesseler; Image 3 © Michael Heath / Alamy; Image 4 © Jonathan Wilson / Alamy. An Epping Forest Circular: Image 1 © IwonaWawro; Image 2 © Alexey Fedorenko / Adobe Stock; Image 3 © Marco Kesseler. Crystal Palace to Nunhead Cemetery: Image 1 © Marco Kesseler; Image 2 © Jansos / Alamy. The Wandle Trail: © Malcolm Park / Alamy © Peter Trimming © Oliver Smart / Alamy © Malcolm Park / Alamy. Richmond Park Circular: Image 1 © Simon Wilkes; Image 2 © Lana2011; Image 3 © Johan Mouchet; Image 4 & 5 © Chanel Irvine. Southbank to City: Image 1 © India Roper-Evans; Image 2 © incamerastock / Alamy; Image 3 © Taran Wilkhu; Image 4 © Mark6138 | Dreamstime.com; Image 5 & 6 © Taran Wilkhu; Image 7 © Georg Eiermann; Image 8 © Alev Takil. Greenwich to Blackheath: Image 1 © robertharding / Alamy; Image 2 © Chris Harris / Alamy; Image 3 © dbrnjhrj / Adobe Stock; Imge 4 © JOHN BRACEGIRDLE / Alamy. Thames Path to Kew: Image 1 © RJT Photography / Alamy; Image 2 © Roberto Herrett / Alamy; Image 3 © Arcaid Images / Alamy; Image 4 & 5 © Marco Kesseler. Little Venice to Camden Lock: Image 1 © RJT Photography / Alamy; Image 2 © David Post; Image 3 © Jim Monk / Alamy. Seven Thames Bridge: Image 1 © ViewFromAbove / Alamy; Image 2 © Vlad Ghiea / Alamy; Image 3 © Lorenza Marzocchi. Royal Parks Ramble: Image 1 © Ellie Wicks; Image 2 © Frank Fischbach / Alamy; Image 3 © Peter D Noyce / Alamy; Image 4 © Marco Kesseler. Hampstead and the Heath: Image 1 © David Wilson; Image 2 © Lee Martin / Alamy; Image 3 © David Jacobs / Alamy; Image 4 © Marco Kesseler; Image 5 © Taran Wilkhu. The Parkland Walk: Image 1 © Marco Kesseler; Image 2 © coldsnowstorm; Image 3 © Marco Kesseler.

AUTHOR'S THANKS

Many thanks to Hattie and Ally (my orienteering oracles), Tom, Erin, Su, Dulcie, Andrew, Rachelle, Phoebe, Kate, Leanne and Francie for the company that made the many days on the hoof a convivial rather than solitary endeavour.

Thanks as ever to Dom, Flo, Ann and Martin at Hoxton Mini Press for the opportunity to explore the city's inner nooks and serene outer zones, in what mostly amounted to decent weather.

ABOUT HOXTON MINI PRESS

Hoxton Mini Press is a small independent publisher based in east London. We are committed to making beautiful but affordable books that don't screw up the planet. We offset all our printing, and we hope that the trees we do use will continue their life as books that you'll pass on to your grandchildren.

Selected opinionated guides in the series:

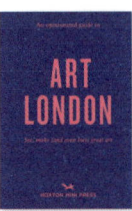